MIZAN SERIES 3

THE END OF MIDDLE EAST HISTORY AND OTHER CONJECTURES

The Mizan Series

The Mizan Series is published by the Ilex Foundation in partnership with the Center for Hellenic Studies. The series supports the central mission of the Mizan digital initiative to encourage informed public discourse and interdisciplinary scholarship on the history, culture, and religion of Muslim societies and civilizations.

www.mizanproject.org

Also in the Mizan Series

Muslim Superheroes: Comics, Islam, and Representation,
edited by A. David Lewis and Martin Lund

Muslims and US Politics Today: A Defining Moment,
edited by Mohammad Hassan Khalil

THE END OF MIDDLE EAST HISTORY
AND OTHER CONJECTURES

by
Richard W. Bulliet

Ilex Foundation
Boston, Massachusetts

Center for Hellenic Studies
Trustees for Harvard University
Washington, D. C.

Distributed by Harvard University Press
Cambridge, Massachusetts and London, England

The End of Middle East History and Other Conjectures
by Richard W. Bullietl

Published by Ilex Foundation, Boston, Massachusetts and The Center for Hellenic Studies, Trustees for Harvard University, Washington, D.C.

Distributed by Harvard University Press, Cambridge, Massachusetts and London, England

Production editor: Christopher Dadian
Cover design: Joni Godlove
Printed in the United States of America

The cover image is from an unpublished manuscript from the southern Philippines.

Library of Congress Cataloging-in-Publication Data

Names: Bulliet, Richard W., author.
Title: The end of Middle East history and other conjectures / Richard W.
    Bulliet.
Other titles: Mizan series ; 3.
Description: Boston, Massachusetts : Ilex Foundation ; Washington, DC :
    Center for Hellenic Studies, Trustees for Harvard University, 2020. |
    Series: Mizan series ; 3 | Includes bibliographical references.
Identifiers: LCCN 2019046329 | ISBN 9780674241336 (paperback)
Subjects: LCSH: Civilization, Arab. | Imaginary histories. | Middle
    East--History.
Classification: LCC DS42.5 .B852 2020 | DDC 956--dc23
LC record available at https://lccn.loc.gov/2019046329

CONTENTS

Preface: Conjectures

"AHA!" MOMENTS IN LIFE come unexpectedly and may not be grasped fully at the time. The first I can remember took place in 1959 during a lecture on Chinese geography that Harvard professor John King Fairbank was giving at the beginning of an East Asian History survey course.

Red China being enemy territory at that time, Fairbank was using old, black-and-white, pre-World War II slides to tell us about Chinese agriculture. The slide showed a huge conical mound of a dark substance surrounded by a scattering of farmers and a few village houses. He told us that the substance was nightsoil, that is, human waste collected from urban latrines to be spread on the fields as fertilizer. The next slide showed the same farmers and the same village houses surrounding a dozen or so smaller cones of the same dark substance. "When you have collected enough nightsoil," said Fairbank, "you can divide it into smaller piles."

I don't know when it struck me that these two slides constituted a metaphor for the scholarly enterprise. When enough data has been piled together, it can be divided into smaller piles. Scholarship lies in assembling the data, to be sure, but the greater test lies in deciding how the division into smaller piles should be carried out and how the smaller piles relate to each other. If this is not done well, your data is just shit.

Things relate to each other in many different ways, of course. A theory postulates a relationship, or a type of relationship, that further research may disprove, modify, or show to be robust. As crucial as theories are, however, they are often rooted in conjectures, and many conjectures are not susceptible of proof. The Latin origin of the word "conjecture" suggests things being thrown together (*con-* "together" + *iactus* "thrown") to see if they make any sense. Hence not much is made of most conjectures. The conjecture that orange hair correlates with egocentric bombast, for example, flits temptingly through the mind but finds nowhere to lodge.

Some conjectures, however, are more conducive to fresh ideas and serious reflection than are fully articulated theories. Conjectures like Heaven, Hell, and divine punishment, for example, or Thomas Hobbes's state of nature and Jean-Jacques Rousseau's social contract: all unprovable conjectures, but ones upon which great edifices have been built.

Other conjectures border on fantasy. Alternate histories, for example, are by definition unprovable conjectures. Yet a great deal of thought, much (most?) of it silly, to be sure, has been prompted by people trying to imagine how history would have been different if Hitler had won World War

II, Jefferson Davis's Confederacy had prevailed in the Civil War, or Charles Martel had lost his life to the Muslim invaders of Europe at the Battle of Tours. Conjectures about the future are similarly unprovable, by definition, even though the profession of futurology and the vogue for apocalyptic fiction thrive on the thoughts they inspire.

Successful scholarly careers are frequently founded on a conjecture conceived during one's college years. Graduate research transforms it into a full-fledged theory subject to substantiation in a doctoral thesis. This then becomes the scholar's first book, which sometimes contains the only fresh idea that he or she will ever come up with. Mathematicians and physical scientists are notoriously portrayed as people whose greatest work, based on some breakthrough conjecture, is behind them by the time they are thirty years old. Historians are granted a few extra decades to think of something exciting before passing to their maker unrewarded.

In my own case, a peculiar turn of mind has granted me a seemingly endless stream of conjecture. Science fiction, fantasy, surrealism, and lucid dreaming furnish many rooms in my mental home and have contributed to an assortment of novels and artworks. More importantly, my conjectures as a historian have led me into unexplored byways of real or imagined pasts and futures. Most of my scholarly publishing has been rooted in "Aha!" moments.

The essays collected in this volume are all conjectural. They range from an alternative history transpiring from a conjectural Ottoman conquest of Vienna in 1529, to a conjectured trajectory of Middle Eastern history in the twenty-first century, to a fantasized account of the evolution of birds from dinosaurs. Some of the conjectures, such as my thoughts on the origin of civilization, are ones that I had once hoped to develop into full-fledged theories and argue at length. At age 76, however, I recognize that the decade or so such an enterprise might take extends well beyond my likely lifespan.

I hope that my readers will be entertained by what I have included here, some of the essays having been published before in less accessible locations. Beyond that, I hope that one or two might be stimulated by one or another of my conjectures to push the ideas forward into undiscovered territory.

ISLAM AND THE MIDDLE EAST

The End of Middle East History
(unchanged from 2013)

Part One

I RECENTLY COMPLETED forty years teaching the history of the Middle East. Inspired by a middle-of-the-night sense of clairvoyance after my penultimate class, I devoted my final lecture to recounting the history of the Middle East in the twenty-first century as seen looking backward from the year 2099. By that date, I foresaw, the idea of a coherent geographical area called the Middle East, an area which had come into being in the maelstrom of three world wars, two hot and one cold, had become obsolete. Hence, its history could be laid out as a closed episode in the global flow of events. The following essay recounts how the history of the Middle East ended.

Central to my hindsight was the untying of the Israel-Palestine knot, a process that took place over a span of years when the Jews and Arabs of Israel/Palestine gradually started to look more to the future than to the past. Both the "two-state solution," which so many Palestinians had seen as permanent subjection to the Israeli boot, and the "one-state solution," which so many Jews had seen as an Arab demographic time-bomb destined to explode the Zionist dream, lost momentum when it became obvious that neither side would ever be ready to surrender. In their place both sides began to consider the idea of a bicommunal State of Israel.

Despite its fifteen-year civil war, brought on primarily by military weakness and external meddling and intervention, Lebanon was taken as a conceptual model. In 1943, with post-war independence from French colonial rule an almost tangible dream, Lebanon's leaders had crafted a way of managing the sometimes murderous sectarian strife that had troubled their society for more than two centuries. The Maronites, the most populous Christian sect, surrendered their ardently held aspiration to remain separate from the Arab world as protégés of France. The Sunnis, the most populous Muslim sect, forswore their equally ardent nationalist aspiration to unite Arab Lebanon with its larger Syrian neighbor. Instead, the Lebanese agreed that their land should be a separate and independent Arab country with a strictly defined governmental balance in which the Christians would retain, at least formally, their majority status.

Based on the fact that the Maronite community had been the most numerous in the census of 1932, the presidency of the republic was accorded in perpetuity to a Maronite Christian. The second largest community, the Sunnis, gained the prime ministry, in perpetuity. The post of Speaker of the National Assembly went to the third largest community, the Shi'ites, the deputy speakership to the Greek Orthodox Christians, and so forth through the major governing offices. As for the National Assembly, the leaders agreed that Christian members should always outnumber Muslims in a ratio of 6 to 5. Elections were to be communally unified so that Christians would vote for Muslim candidates along with representatives of their own communities on combined slates, and vice versa. It was further agreed that the census figures of 1932 would not be up-dated, at least for the purpose of apportioning power, even though they were bound to change because of differing emigration patterns and birth rates.

Lebanon's leaders had not been alone in thinking constitutionally along communal lines. A few years earlier when the northern Syrian province of Hatay had been in the process of being transferred to Turkish sovereignty, an assembly with fixed demographically based representations of Turks, Alawites, Arabs, Armenians, and others had been visualized.

In my look backward from 2099, Israel's Jews and the Palestinian Arabs living in Israel, the West Bank, and the Gaza Strip finally saw the futility of trying to resolve past injustices and retaliate for past acts of bloodshed and began to think about the state that might come into being through a bicommunal constitution: a State of Israel that would not only be politically accepted by the Arab world, but would also have the region's most dynamic economy and unmatchable military superiority.

What they came up with – needless to say, after years of wrangling and anguishing internal debate – was the following:

The Jews gave up defining Israel as the homeland of all the world's Jews in return for a constitutionally fixed majority role in a bicommunal state. Whatever might happen in terms of immigration or birthrate differentials, Israel's Jews would never be inundated or outvoted by the country's Arab citizens. In that respect, Israel would retain a preponderantly Jewish government. But Israel would no longer be defined as a Jewish state. The painful relinquishing of this fundamental identity came as the force of the Zionist dream of Israel as a refuge for a world Jewish community plagued by European anti-Semitism diminished. With rancor against Israel's uncompromising attitude toward the Palestinians constituting the core of anti-Semitic feelings around the world, escape to Israel no longer meant what it had meant in the 1930s. Jews as such were statistically more likely to be killed or injured by deliberate violence in their own state of Israel than in any other country.

In Europe and the United States in particular, the universal post-Holocaust affirmation that Judeo-Christian values formed the basis of Western civilization had greatly attenuated traditions of anti-Semitism that stretched back for many centuries.

For their part, the Palestinians made the equally wrenching decision to give up the idea of eradicating Jewish political strength and along with it the hope of attaining sovereign control over an Arab Palestinian state large enough and viable enough to satisfy their aspiration for independence and national pride. Despite, or, in the thinking of some, because of, the inevitability of the Arab population of Israel and the occupied territories eventually outnumbering the Jewish population, they realized not only that the Jews would never give up what they had achieved during the decades of Israel's existence as a Jewish state, but also that without those Jewish achievements, an independent Palestine would scarcely be viable.

After each side had put aside its maximal aspirations, the two parties decided to balance, in token form, their ideological obligations to their respective diasporas. The Law of Return that guaranteed citizenship to Jews immigrating to Israel from the diaspora was paired with a Right of Return for Palestinians living in exile since 1948. On the assumption that every new citizen accepted under the Law of Return came with a family, or intended to start one, it was agreed that for every Jewish immigrant granted Israeli citizenship, the descendants of one Palestinian nuclear family from the 1948 diaspora would be offered an opportunity to return and settle in some part of the now combined territories of Israel, the West Bank, and the Gaza Strip.

Haggling over the precise communal balance in a bicommunal constitution required a lot of diplomatic hand-holding by sympathetic parties, but this helped guarantee that the final agreement had broad international acceptance. Eventually, leaders of the Israeli Jewish community and the Palestinian Arab community agreed on the following governmental structure:

The largely ceremonial presidency of the bicommunal State of Israel would forever go to an Arab. Unlike the Lebanese precedent, where the most populous community gained the presidency, this assignment of office was mainly symbolic. Leaders from both sides agreed that an Arab presidency would confirm Israel's place in the Middle East and the Arab world and abolish the old shibboleth about Israel being a European "colonial-settler state." Though the name Israel was retained in recognition of the Jewish governmental majority, it was no longer defined as a Jewish state.

The office of prime minister, the effective head of government, was fixed as a Jewish position since it was constitutionally guaranteed that the

Knesset would have a permanently guaranteed majority of Jewish members at a ratio of 6 to 5, based roughly on each community's share of the population in 2030. The remaining cabinet ministries were divided half and half. The Minister of Defense was assigned to a Jew because it was recognized that it would take years of painstaking step-by-step progress in training, confidence building, and popular recognition that peace was indeed at hand to move toward an agreed upon goal of integrating Jews and Arabs in the Israel Defense Force. The foreign ministry, on the other hand, initially went to the Arabs since the job of convincing the surrounding Arab countries of the value of the new state structure and thereby ending a century of animosity was seen as the greatest diplomatic task at hand. In the constitution as it was finally adopted, however, the communal assignment of cabinet portfolios below the premiership was not specified beyond the provision that every cabinet would have to include equal numbers of Jewish and Arab members and be approved by two-thirds of the Knesset.

As for elections, as in Lebanon, members of the parliament were to be elected by districts in ratios appropriate to the communal preponderance in each district. All voters would be offered ballots with mixed Arab-Jewish slates of names identified by party, or by party alliances in which Jewish parties would share slates with Arab parties.

With Jerusalem the undivided capital of the bicommunal republic and the pre-1967 boundaries rendered obsolete by the unification of the territories, controversies concerning Jewish settlements and the sharing of land, water, and resources subsided. A bicommunal commission was established to dismantle long-standing discriminatory practices and institutions. Six months after the new constitution went into effect, the barrier built to curb Palestinian violence was taken down. The rate of progress in working out the bicommunal structure and eliminating deeply engrained structures of inequality was too slow for some, and too fast for others. But progress was made, and a new state of affairs in the Middle East was slowly recognized by the time of the centennial of the Six Day War in 2067.

As the idea of a bicommunal state progressed over the years from fanciful notion, to real possibility, to constitutional reality, the potential consequences of such a development became a preoccupation not just for the Palestinians and the Jews, but for every country, party, and movement that had a history of involvement with the Israel-Palestine dilemma.

Not surprisingly, the members of the Gulf Cooperation Council were the first Arab countries to embrace the new concept. Palestinian resistance to Israel had never been the consuming passion there that it had been for the so-called frontline Arab states. Kuwait's expulsion of its Palestinian community in 1991 on charges of collaboration with Saddam Hussein's brutal occupation had made this crystal clear. The Gulf region's comparative isolation from the Israel-Palestine cockpit helped the GCC recognize the great and mutual advantages to be gained by combining Gulf petroleum resources and capital with Israel's industrial and business know-how and scientific expertise. Arab businesses based in Israel, many of them emerging first as subsidiaries of Jewish companies, easily formed commercial ties with companies and government agencies in Kuwait, UAE, Bahrain, Qatar, and Oman, though Saudi Arabia was a bit slower to respond to the new opportunities.

What turned the tide with respect to the Saudis was the American reaction to the growing pace of Arab-Jewish cooperation in Israel. Despite several decades of earnest political declarations, handwringing by pundits, and periodic spikes in oil prices, the United States had proven incapable of stifling its thirst for Persian Gulf oil. Yet friction arising from the stationing of American military forces in Qatar, Bahrain, and Iraq on what seemed destined, in the eyes of both Americans and America's detractors, to become a permanent basis grew steadily worse. Despite repeated presidential disclaimers of any imperialist intent in prolonging the military presence that began with the first Gulf war of 1991, the United States came increasingly to be seen, both at home and abroad, as an unwelcome colonial presence in the region. Nevertheless, the halting but generally peaceful course of governmental institution building in Iraq seemed to preclude a complete American withdrawal. In the eyes of Washington policy-makers, training and counterterrorism units continued to be needed within that country, and American control of Iraqi and Gulf airspace still seemed indispensable.

The idea of replacing American military units with Israeli units was greeted at first as an absurdity. But as the formation of effective Arab military units with Arab officers within the Israel Defense Force became a reality, the realization spread that a first-class Israeli Arab military force with Arab officers in local command could substitute for the increasingly unwelcome Americans. Israeli Arab colonels and generals quickly showed that they could interact efficiently with both indigenous Gulf commanders and a shrinking core of American advisors. Israel's nuclear umbrella and state-of-the-art mastery of Gulf airspace, all implemented in close collaboration with the GCC military commands, finally allowed the Americans to go home. Moreover, the power to forestall the ambitions of the Islamic Republic of Iran (IRI) shifted from American to Arab hands, albeit with the United States maintaining its commitment to keep the IDF supplied with the latest weapons systems.

The emerging Dubai-Jerusalem axis overturned many of the assumptions that had driven Arab politics in the days of the Arab-Israel conflict. Egypt, Jordan, Syria, and Lebanon, the erstwhile frontline states, were barred by Israel's new constitution from forming political linkages with the reconceived bicommunal state. At the same time, they lost their claim to financial support from their oil-rich Arab cousins based on confronting, or confronting in the past, the Zionist entity.

Meanwhile, economic stagnation and the deficits in human resource development first documented in turn-of-the-century United Nations reports had deepened with the passage of time. So had regime suppression of popular discontent over national decline and neo-Mamluk authoritarianism. This oppression had long been buttressed by American assumptions that Arab-Israel peace hinged on the cooperation of Israel's neighbors. The United States had consistently expressed only token support for political liberalization, and this had made hatred of the United States as the evil facilitator of Arab totalitarianism a fundamental tenet of Islamic extremist ideology.

However, as the Palestinians and the Israeli Jews inched toward their historic settlement, the United States came to realize that it no longer needed to guarantee the survival of militaristic rule in the neighboring countries. Political instability in Syria, Egypt, Jordan, or Lebanon would no longer threaten what domestic American political forces had long deemed a vital American interest: the security of Israel. The new Israel that was in the making would be more than capable of taking care of itself. So American policy-makers began to distance themselves from the neo-Mamluk autocrats and push for open elections.

Recognizing that without an unwelcome and discriminatory Jewish state to excite popular passions and coerce the United States into rubber-stamping its oppressive policies, the nascent Assad and Mubarak [*sic*] dynasties in Syria and Egypt and the genuine Hashimite dynasty in Jordan succumbed to the tide of history. While keeping a measure of authority in the hands of the military and the president or king, they cautiously introduced pluralist electoral reforms. This led to parliamentary pluralities for Islamist parties, and those parties promptly demonstrated that they were not yet ready to govern. Parliaments were accordingly dissolved by the central authorities. But after several cycles of government malfeasance and fresh elections, the Islamist parties began to learn the ropes. It took some twenty years for open parliamentary systems to stabilize, but internal discontent subsided much sooner as Egyptians, Syrians, and Jordanians responded positively to life in a freer society. For the first time since the heyday of Arab revolutionary regimes in the 1960s, people in the central Arab states regained some hope for the future. King Hussein of Jordan was often cited as a model for his short-lived attempt to allow Islamists to participate in his country's electoral system in the early 1990s. Ironically, however, considering the abject failure of the Bush administration's fantasy of catalyzing region-wide democratic change by means of military invasion, the Arab world found a better model in the post-American political evolution of the Iraqi republic, where parties that had originally formed around religious ideologies gradually gained sophistication in the arts of winning elections and governing equitably. Iraq's experience became an informal roadmap for a general dismantling of neo-Mamluk autocracy.

Since the political problems that had sparked Lebanon's civil war had been caused by external interference rather than domestic authoritarianism, Lebanon capitalized rather easily on the emergence of the new Israel. Lebanese bankers were happy to lend their expertise to forging Israel-Arab commercial linkages. Hizbullah lost its rationale of protecting the Shi'ite south from Israeli invasion and turned in its guns. But by the time this happened it had already established itself as one of the country's most sophisticated political parties. Syrian interference in Lebanon's affairs became a distant memory as concern with internal political development became that country's primary preoccupation. No longer in need of Syrian and Iranian military support, Hizbullah helped the Syrians get over their Lebanese obsession.

The new bicommunal Israel, in tandem with the economically cooperating states of the GCC, transformed the eastern Arab world. Powerful, dynamic, and constitutionally balanced, it became the state that every other state wanted to befriend rather than attack. And this spelled the end of the ill-starred Iranian notion of playing a power role in the Arab world.

Part Two

Iran's Arab adventure had ostensibly grown from three separate roots, Islamic revolution, Shi'ite solidarity, and sympathy for the Palestinians. But underlying each of these was a dream dating back to the overthrow of Prime Minister Mossadegh in 1953, the dream of confronting and confounding American imperial arrogance. Now each of the three roots withered, and confrontation with the Great Satan faded from significance along with them.

The idea of an Islamic revolution leading to an Islamic republic that would reinvigorate the faith and reveal the viciousness of Western stereotypes of Islam had lost steam before the IRI was a decade old. Internal progress had been stifled by eight years of war with Iraq and by factional infighting that sapped governmental innovation and efficiency. Though public discourse of unprecedented vitality flourished after the revolution, other intellectual and philosophical trends superseded the concept of Islamic revolution per se. However, the death knell of constructive Islamic revolution was rung on September 11, 2001 when the terrorist attacks on the World Trade Center and the Pentagon elevated nihilistic violence in the name of (Sunni) Islam above the dream of creating a model religious state in (Shiʿite) Iran. Instead of an Islamic republic, the ideologues of the new terrorism called for an autocratic Islamic emirate or an atavistic return to a universal caliphate that had not wielded significant political power for over a thousand years. In response, Islamic political parties everywhere put behind them the idea of an Islamic republic, and with it the Iranian model, and called instead for pluralistic electoral systems in which Islamist parties would be free to run for office, but not free to disempower rival non-religious parties.

The second root of Iran's Arab policy, justice for the Palestinians, had long been subject to the condition that whatever the Palestinians themselves agreed to by way of a settlement with Israel would be accepted by the Islamic Republic of Iran. Thus the negotiations for a bicommunal state of Israel spelled the end of Iran's courting of Arab public opinion. When Hamas signed on to the new constitutional order, which did not require it to disavow its rejection of a definitionally Jewish state, Iran had no choice but to go along. And the same was true of Hizbullah, Iran's Lebanese proxy.

Hizbullah, however, enjoyed Iranian support not just because of its resistance to Israel but also because of its representation of Shiʿite political claims within the Lebanese system. Throughout the saber-rattling era when the United States and the old Israel strove with all their might to demonize Iran, the specter of an Iran-led Shiʿite alliance bringing to an end a millennium of Sunni dominance had been deployed unsuccessfully in an effort to persuade Sunni Arab popular opinion that fear of one's Shiʿite neighbor took precedence over support for the beleaguered Palestinians.

A geographically strained fantasy had conjured up the specter of the Lebanese Shiʿite minority, spearheaded by Hizbullah, connecting through Syria (inconveniently a predominantly Sunni country) with a dominant (but not overwhelming) Shiʿite political establishment in Iraq. When bits and pieces of support in Bahrain and the eastern province of Saudi Arabia were added in, this phantasm was portrayed as becoming potent enough to nullify the overwhelmingly Sunni majorities in Egypt, the Arabian peninsula, Turkey, Jordan, Palestine, and, of course, Syria. This absurdity rested entirely on the notion that an Islamic Republic of Iran armed with nuclear weapons could force the Sunni world to kowtow to the Hidden Imam. Yet no one ever proposed an actual strategy for Iran using nuclear weapons to this end. It was absurd enough to imagine Iran embracing regime suicide by initiating a grossly asymmetrical nuclear exchange with the old Israel. But Iran bombing Cairo? Riyadh? Abu Dhabi? The notion was ridiculous on its face, which made it doubly ridiculous when Sunni Arab regimes courted American and Israeli favor by saying how greatly they feared Iran's Shi'ite juggernaut.

As it turned out, once the Palestinians resolved their issues with the Israelis, Iran accepted their decision, and the appeal of the Islamic Republic to the Arab street began to fade. Without this hook into Arab public opinion, and with an Islamic republican form of government that had failed to impress the Muslim world, shared Shi'ite belief became a weak rationale for Iran continuing to interfere in Arab political affairs. As for the goal underlying so much of the IRI's foreign policy, confronting American arrogance, this too waned as American forces executed an orderly withdrawal from Iraq and plans were announced for Arab troops from the new IDF to take on security responsibility for the Arab Gulf. These plans took many years to accomplish in full, but long before then Iran took note of the changing geopolitical climate and executed a momentous turn away from the Middle East.

Ever since the opening of Silk Road trade to China around the third century BCE, Iran's fortunes had depended far more on events taking place to the north and east than on those taking place to the west. Though Alexander the Great had conquered Iran from the west in pre-Silk Road times, and the Arab armies of Islam were to do so again in the seventh century CE, Iran's mountainous borders with Iraq and Turkey made it largely invulnerable to conquest from the west. Its eastern frontier, however, was porous. Scythians, Hephthalites, Oghuz Turks, Mongols, Uzbeks, and Afghans invaded with comparative ease on different occasions. Similarly, Khazar Turks, Georgians, and Russians periodically threatened from the northwest. For its own part, Iran's westward military ambitions aimed less at conquest than at protecting the country from Ottoman invasion. But to the north and east, Iran repeatedly sought aggrandizement with powerful monarchs marching again and again into Afghanistan, India, Central Asia, and Georgia.

This military track record was hardly surprising given Iran's linguistic and ethnic linkages. Persian, the native language of about half of Iran's population, was closely related to languages spoken in Afghanistan, Tajikistan, and Pakistan while Azerbaijani Turkish, Iran's second most common tongue, was even more closely related to the languages of Turkey, Azerbaijan, Turkmenistan, Uzbekistan, Kyrgyzstan, and Kazakhstan. By comparison, Arabic speakers in Iran amounted to only three percent of the population, and Persian was nowhere spoken in the Arab lands.

When the term "the Middle East" had become common in both scholarly and popular usage after World War II, Iran had been included as an integral part of the region despite its many dissimilarities. This was because the Cold War division of the world into regions was based on the geopolitics of imperialism more than on language, religion, ethnicity, economics, or geography. For all practical purposes, "The Middle East" was defined as the area to the west of British India, to the east of French North Africa, and to the south of the Stans, the Muslim lands incorporated into the Soviet Union. More importantly, it was a region believed to be endangered by Soviet expansion and communist subversion. Iran, in its Shi'ism, its never having been part of the Ottoman Empire, its relative independence during the post-World War I period when French and British imperialists were humiliating the Arab world, and eventually its Islamic revolution, had little in common with the other countries of the region it was assigned to.

Oil, exceptionally, was a shared preoccupation. But countries that were blessed with sufficient oil reserves to become major exporters had no intrinsic tie to one another beyond a common interest in nationalizing their oil industries and maintaining high levels of production and profit. In these respects, Iran did indeed have interests in common with Iraq, Saudi Arabia, and the Gulf emirates, but also with Venezuela, Indonesia, Mexico, and Nigeria. Oil was not a Middle East thing.

Iran's reassessment of its geopolitical situation in response to the progress being made in the Israel-Palestine arena took the form of looking to the east and the north. Russia and China had won Iran's confidence by protecting it from devastating international sanctions over its nuclear program. India and Pakistan were in dire need of pipeline access to oil and gas from Iran and the Stans. Afghanistan was a serious security concern because of its seemingly endless instability, deeply engrained Taliban animosity toward Shi'ism, and the flood of opium smuggled across its Iranian border. All of these factors contributed to Iran's growing orientation toward the countries of the Shanghai Cooperation Organization (SCO).

At its outset in 2001, the SCO had brought together Russia, China, Kazakhstan, Tajikistan, Uzbekistan, and Turkmenistan in a series of mutual security agreements. But its perspective had soon expanded to encompass international trade matters, and representatives from Iran, Pakistan, India, and Mongolia began to attend its meetings as observers. With the Chinese, Indian, and to a lesser degree Russian economies among the first to recover from the Great Recession of the Obama years, the idea took hold of consolidating the relations adumbrated by the SCO and thus stealing an economic march on the still languishing European Union and the United States. Russia, China, India, and Iran became the four anchors of a regional bloc that encompassed the world's most dynamic economies, largest domestic markets, and most abundant untapped sources of minerals and hydrocarbons.

Though Iran was the smallest of the big four, its role was pivotal, as was that of the United States. Building on the trust gained from cooperating in Afghan security matters and in appreciation of Iran's hands-off policy toward Iraq, the Obama administration had used the carrot of lifting American obstacles to pipeline building to wring from Iran a commitment, subject to verification, to freeze its long-range missile program and never assemble or test a nuclear weapon. The resulting Iranian pipeline ventures from the Caspian region to Pakistan and India brought Iran into the heart of the SCO structure. Though instability continued to be endemic in the ungovernable mountain core of what came to be thought of as Pakghanistan, the new sources of energy and political cooperation helped the Islamabad government recover its equilibrium.

Nevertheless, SCO collaboration fell far short of what was achieved by the EU, with its fifty-year head start. Once through the Great Recession, the Europeans finally agreed to admit Turkey as a member. Twenty years later they admitted Morocco and Tunisia and agreed to candidacy status for Algeria. Behind the opening toward North Africa was a growing realization that the grandchildren of the veiled or bearded Muslim immigrants of the late twentieth century had become pretty much indistinguishable from other Europeans, and that North Africa would continue to be the best source of labor for European economies beset by low birth rates and large populations of retirees. Just as Turkey had instituted innumerable reforms to meet the EU's political, economic, and social standards, so the Moroccans and Tunisians, and more reluctantly the Algerians, opened their political systems and adopted EU-stipulated corrective policies.

As the twenty-first century neared its end, Turkey, Morocco, and Tunisia were firmly a part of the European orbit, and Algeria was headed in the same direction. At the other end of the old Middle East, Iran was firmly a part of the SCO orbit. As for the eastern Arab world, it formed an orbit of its own based on the financial and petroleum resources of the Gulf and the military, commercial, and scientific dynamism of the bicommunal Israeli state. The other Arab states of the region attached themselves as best they could to the Jerusalem-Dubai axis.

Apart from these political transformations, the century also witnessed remarkable changes in the world Islamic community. Iran's Islamic revolution had proven a false dawn. Though important amendments to the Islamic Republic's constitution had been made after the death of Ayatollah Khomeini, it took two more rounds of amendments to make the political system workable. The obstructive power of the Guardian Council and various ambiguities concerning the authority of the Governing Religious Jurist were the targets of the reformers. But the intrinsically Shi'ite character of the Jurist's role prevented the IRI from being regarded as a model anywhere in the Sunni world.

As for the perpetrators and theoreticians of revolutionary or jihadist violence in the name of Islam, changes in the political arena greatly lessened their appeal to ordinary Muslims. Agreement on a bicommunal Israel not only eliminated the perennial fear of Jewish oppression and expansion, but it also brought to the fore a new generation of influential Arab leaders dedicated to moving beyond the bad old days of war and intifada. Similarly, the American withdrawal from Iraq and plans for a transfer of security responsibility in the Persian Gulf, combined with a reversal of the American commitment to the survival of neo-Mamluk Arab regimes, took the anti-American wind from al-Qaeda's sails. Militant groups continued to train and operate in remote locales in Pakghanistan, Somalia, and elsewhere, but the tide of violence had clearly begun to ebb by 2025.

New measures to reinstitutionalize religious authority within Sunni Islam contributed as much to rolling back the tide of violence as the more obvious political developments. Authoritarian regimes, some of neo-Mamluk and some of monarchical character, had originally contributed to the decline of Sunni religious authority by forcing conformity on their scholarly Muslim establishments and at the same time educating a new generation of politically aware and technically capable citizens. The resulting loss of respect for the traditional scholarly authorities had made room for a diversity of ambitious Muslims, many of them with only limited expertise in religious matters, to propagate militant views among a discontented public.

The oppressive responses of the authoritarian rulers had fallen heavily on moderates who wanted to accomplish their religiously inspired political programs through electoral and parliamentary means. This rejection of moderation had discouraged many citizens and thereby empowered the violent end of the Islamist political spectrum. The gradual opening of the political systems in the authoritarian states now reversed that process. Moderate Islamist democrats working with some credible hope for success attracted popular followings, and the advocates of violence and revolution lost ground accordingly.

Turkey, Indonesia, and Malaysia led the way in creating fully democratic majority Muslim polities with Morocco, Tunisia, and Algeria following more slowly under the goad of EU accession. As for the Muslim diaspora in Europe and the Americas, new educational and intellectual initiatives fostered firm convictions that minority status in pluralist and structurally secular polities was acceptable according to well-reasoned interpretations of Muslim law and tradition. In an effort to diminish friction between old Islamic intellectual centers, such as Egypt and Saudi Arabia, and the new ideas emerging in diaspora and Asian Muslim communities, the Organization of the Islamic Conference [later, Organization of Islamic Cooperation] took the lead in organizing new forums for sharing ideas about Islam and identifying areas of consensus and areas where different communities might respectfully agree to disagree.

This diffusion of Muslim religious authority to diaspora, minority, and geographically peripheral (from the point of view of Egypt and Saudi Arabia) communities cannot be considered the final step in the dissolution of the concept of the Middle East because it took place in stages as the more dramatic political changes were taking shape. But it constituted an essential element. Though "the Middle East" of the Cold War era had been constructed in response to the vagaries of western imperialism, there had always been a common sense understanding that the historical center of Islam, including the territories that had once made up the medieval caliphate, had a legitimate claim to being the territorial focus of a worldwide Muslim community. But in the twenty-first century, the Muslim community finally became as global in thought and authority as it long had been in faith.

So the Middle East disappeared. North Africa and Turkey went with Europe. Iran went with Asia. The eastern Arab world revolved around a new axis running from Jerusalem to Dubai. And the world's Muslims found ways of leading religiously fulfilling lives wherever they happened to live.

Critiquing Orientalism:
Marshall Hodgson and Edward Said
(2017)

TWO LANDMARKS of late twentieth-century thought on Islam and the Middle East: Edward Said's *Orientalism* was published in 1978; Marshall Hodgson's three-volume *The Venture of Islam: Conscience and History in a World Civilization* was published in 1974, six years after its author's death. I doubt that Said and Hodgson ever met or that either was aware of the other's project. Yet both books, from different standpoints, address the quality of European understandings or misunderstandings of the Muslim world. Said impugns the mindsets of the French and English writers and artists he surveys. Hodgson seeks to correct what he sees as their flawed foundational ideas but works to erect a grander and more coherent edifice on the ones he deems sound.

Scholars who were working in the field in the1970s were buffeted by the challenges Said and Hodgson presented. Both authors broke so strongly from the preceding conventions of scholarship on Islam, exemplified by the likes of Ignaz Goldziher and H. A. R. Gibb along with the collective efforts of the contributors to the *Encyclopedia of Islam*, that they could not be ignored. Students entering the field from the 1980s onward, however, generally reacted to their ideas according to the positive or negative appreciations that were telegraphed to them by their teachers. It is worth recalling, therefore, who Hodgson and Said were and what their intellectual landmarks looked like when they first appeared and had not yet been canonized. Beyond that one can offer conjectures as to what they would have made of one another's project.

Marshall Hodgson

I was invited in 2014 to contribute a paper on Hodgson's neologism *islamicate* and discuss its impact on my own work for a conference at the University of Chicago, where Hodgson had taught and inspired a coterie of students. The rationale for the conference was the fortieth anniversary of the publication of *The Venture of Islam*, but it was also an opportunity for direct and indirect students and admirers of Hodgson to make laudatory speeches.

In the event, I could not attend the conference and thus avoided revisiting the reservations about Hodgson's work I had first aired, to the displeasure of his students, in a review of the newly published volumes. *The Venture of Islam* did not intersect my own approach to the field of Islamic history, which was already set by 1974. Having published *The Patricians of Nishapur* and being then in the process of completing *The Camel and the Wheel*, I was fully committed to working on social and economic history and was reasonably satisfied with the conventional vocabulary that reserved "Islamic" for matters pertaining to religion, and "Muslim" for the outlooks and activities of populations that identified, either by faith or cultural style, with that religion. "Islamicate" struck me as not just an unfamiliar word, but also as an unnecessary one. So I have never used it.

My view on this was doubtless shaped by the fact that I was not unfamiliar with Marshall Hodgson as an Islamic history professor. A decade earlier, in the autumn of 1964, he had taught as a visiting professor at Harvard in the place of Professor H. A. R. Gibb, who had suffered a stroke. As it happened, I was due to take my PhD orals, and Hodgson substituted for Gibb as my examiner in the field of Islamic history. My exposure to him, therefore, was not in the context of his writing or teaching, but in that of preparing an examination field.

My first meeting with Hodgson strongly influenced my subsequent view of him as a historian. He asked me what I thought Islamic history consisted of as a field of study. I replied that, to me, Islamic history was the narrative of what could be determined from extant sources concerning events in Muslim ruled lands that transpired from the time of the Prophet down to the Mongol invasion. To this he responded forcefully that I was mistaken. Islamic history, he told me, was the aggregate of what had been thought and written by the great European Orientalists. (These are very close to his exact words.) As the conversation proceeded, he remarked that he had been fluent in French and German when he graduated from high school, and he asked me whether I had read the *opera minora* of Carlo Alfonso Nallino. I told him that I had looked at Nallino's nine volumes of articles in Italian in Widener Library, but had not read them. Moreover, I had no intention of reading them, though I had read a French translation of one book by Nallino on early Arabic literature.

On the basis of this, a few other similarly awkward face-to-face experiences, and his stupendously inept reading of a Quranic passage in his lecture course, I conceived of Hodgson as a person who was in thrall to a tradition of European scholarship on Islam that I myself did not think very highly of. I thought, for example, that Gibb, Harvard's great man in the field, was a masterful Arabist, but too reliant on appraisals of moral worth or delinquency to be a very good historian. (Gibb may very well have defined Islamic history in a way similar to what Hodgson told me, but I never had an opportunity to discuss field readings with him.) As a result, when *The Venture of Islam* was published, I saw it as an impressively deep and critical commentary on European oriental studies, but as having little to say about what I regarded as the most important aspects of Islamic history. Hodgson's neologisms did not strike me as terribly useful; his labels for chronological divisions of Islamic history seemed inconsistent and ill-founded; and the comparative paucity of footnotes guiding readers to texts in Middle Eastern languages bespoke, I thought, the author's greater interest in Islamic history as a domain of European thought than as the story of what happened in the Middle East and North Africa between 600 and 1300.

As for social and economic history, my own fascination, I focused on a passage in Volume III where Hodgson opined that history can be approached in three ways: a narration of events (the *l'histoire événementielle* of the *Annales* school); an account of the interplay of social and economic influences (more or less the *conjunctures* of the *Annales* school); and the story of how dissident individuals of great conscience, al-Hallaj and Ahmad b. Hanbal, for example, change the course of history. The first of these approaches he dismissed as one damn thing after another; the second, he wrote, needed to be followed to the last "cynical" conclusion regarding the forces involved. Truly significant history, however, lay with the third approach, which I eventually came to see as being less a restatement of Hegel's idea of "world historical" individuals, who, after all, were more often conquerors than men of conscience, than as an affirmation of Hodgson's own strong commitment to his Quaker beliefs.

I very much resented Hodgson's application of the word "cynical" to the study of social and economic history, though I suppose in a more extensive conversation he might have couched his misgivings more gently in terms of social historians paying too little attention to individual agency in history. As for the great man of conscience approach, I was not at all interested. Great men of any description have never interested me.

As my own career proceeded, I paid little or no attention to Hodgson's work and rarely assigned it. Thus I find myself today rather surprised by the prominence it has attained. My own research trajectory focused on the question of how conversion to Islam occurred in various lands and what difference it made in the social, political, and economic patterns of life in those lands. This led me away from the heyday of Abbasid rule in Baghdad, Hodgson's "High Caliphate," during which time, according to my calculations, most people in the lands of the caliphate had still not converted to Islam and were still living, if we are given to neologisms, in "Christianate,"

"Judeate," or "Zoroastrianate" rather than "Islamicate" societies, and toward the tenth, eleventh, and twelfth centuries, when they had converted.

Hodgson's chronological focus on the caliphate and on Islamic law (*shariʿa*) struck me as exemplifying what I labeled "the view from the center," a way of approaching Islamic history that focused attention on high culture and political power and neglected "the view from the edge," that is, what was going on in the lives of ordinary people who either lived far from Damascus and Baghdad or did not belong to the literate elite. The chronology that interested me was governed by rates of conversion, with their associated social, economic, and political developments, rather than by fixed political (for example, the caliphate) or military (for example, use of gunpowder) developments.

Ever since the publication of my review of *The Venture of Islam* in 1978, the substance of which I have just summarized, the concern has gnawed at me that my personal relationship with the author, such as it was, imparted a more negative tone to the review than was warranted. While I cannot go back and relive my experiences with Hodgson, I can compare my appraisal with the much more positive one penned by Edmund Burke III, a scholar of deservedly high repute. Burke's essay was published in 1979 under the title "Islamic History as World History: Marshall Hodgson, 'The Venture of Islam'"[1] Burke sees the same shortcomings with Hodgson's writing – congested prose, too many neologisms, occasional crankiness – that I did, but he feels that the overall structure of the book as coded in its subtitle largely redeems them.

Since I have been engaged through seven editions now in writing World History in the form of the textbook *The Earth and Its Peoples: A Global History*,[2] I cannot agree with this judgment. Burke writes:

> Long before the current impasse of the orientalist tradition had become glaringly evident, Hodgson was already convinced of the need for a radical reorientation of our historical and geographical attitudes toward the rest of the world. In my opinion, the effort to write a history of Islamic civilization informed by the multiple awarenesses that derive from such an undertaking constitutes Hodgson's most important achievement. [p. 246]

> Hodgson's attack on the orientalist tradition of scholarship is noteworthy for several reasons. One is that it comes from someone whose training, and in many ways professional self-image, were those of an orientalist. [p. 247]

1. *International Journal of Middle East Studies*, X (1979): 241–64.
2. Seventh edition, Cengage Learning, 2018.

Central to Hodgson's method of doing world history is his use of ideal types to inform and orient his analysis. This gives his study of Islamic civilization an analytical power lacking in other parallel efforts. [p. 249]

That Hodgson was a product of the orientalist tradition that he was bent on reforming is beyond question. But he was also enamored of the Weberian approach to assessing and essentializing civilizations that was widespread in sociological and area studies circles in the 1960s. And this passion for identifying the core ideals of Islam, and hence of Islamic civilization, and extolling some of the most renown religious thinkers ties his world history approach to a broad swath of intellectual endeavor centered on identifying, explaining, and projecting the inevitability of Western modernity and its domination of the globe.

A ... consequence of viewing the rise of the West as a world historical phenomenon is that it enables Hodgson to address the issue of what he calls "the development gap." If the concept is old-fashioned, the insight is contemporary. Once under way, Hodgson argues, the Western Transmutation "could neither be paralleled independently nor be borrowed wholesale." It could also not be escaped. The unprecedented level of social power of the West enabled it to intervene in other societies in countless ways and almost from the beginning to set the terms of its relationship with them. The social basis of civilized life was transformed. [p. 251]

World History as a field of study has advanced substantially since Hodgson's day but has not, for the most part, moved in the direction of identifying the core ideals of civilizations and viewing the rise of Western modernity as a global telos, or even as a good thing. The history of technology, environment, and economic structures is steadily replacing high cultural achievements as the foundation for writing world history. Hodgson's effort to critique the orientalist tradition by placing Islamic civilization within a world historical framework thus runs afoul of evolving preferences of world historians.

As an informed and sharp critique of European scholarship on Islam, however, *The Venture of Islam* deserves to be read and affords a quite different perspective from that of Edward Said.

Edward Said

When I joined the Columbia University faculty in 1976, the full-time Middle East and Islam faculty clustered in the Department of Middle East Languages and Cultures (MELAC). It consisted of three Arabists: Pierre Cachia, an Egyptian-born literature specialist of Maltese background; Maan Madina, a Syrian Kurd who was far more interested in collecting Islamic art than in studying the modern Middle East, his supposed specialty in the department; and Jeanette Wakin, a Lebanese-American specialist on Islamic law. There was also one Persianist, the European-educated Iranian Ehsan Yar-Shater, who was just starting the *Encyclopedia Iranica* project that would be his greatest achievement; and two Turkologists, Tibor Halasi-Kun from Hungary and a British colleague, Kathleen Burrill.

Outside of MELAC, the Egyptian-born economic historian Charles Issawi had absconded to Princeton the year before I arrived. Issawi's departure left Jacob Coleman (J. C. or "Jay") Hurewitz of the Political Science Department as Director and sole full-time faculty member housed in the Middle East Institute, a suite of offices situated in the School of International Affairs, later renamed The School of International and Public Affairs. I moved into Issawi's office because the History Department was cramped for space, and I assumed Issawi's role as co-teacher, with Hurewitz, of a two-semester seminar required for students seeking the Certificate offered by the Institute, a credential analogous to the MA in Middle East Studies then being offered by area studies graduate programs in other universities. Prior to my arrival, Hurewitz had also directed doctoral history theses on the modern Middle East because the historian I replaced, the Scotsman Douglas Dunlop, could not teach effectively outside the medieval period (or, indeed, even within that period).

Historically, Columbia boasted a succession of distinguished Middle East specialists from A. V. W. Jackson, who was named the first occupant of the university's chair in Persian studies in 1895, down to the Australian Semiticist Arthur Jeffery, who died in 1939, and the German specialist on Islamic law, Joseph Schacht, who died in 1969. In 1976, however, the faculty was at a low point so far as publishing distinction in the field was concerned.

No one then had reason to suspect that Columbia's most famous and influential thinker on Middle Eastern matters would prove to be a Palestinian English professor named Edward Said. Said had never taught a course on the Middle East at Columbia, and never would do so down to his death in 2003. And despite many invitations, he never participated in any event or program sponsored by the Middle East Institute. But his book *Orientalism*, published in 1978, had a transformative impact not just on the study Islam and the Middle East, but on intercultural studies of all kinds.

Understandably, Said's blistering critique of Orientalism, which up until that time had been a non-controversial term for scholarship devoted to Asian studies of all sorts, utilized the analytical tools of comparative literature. He surveyed English and French writings on Islam and the Middle East since 1750, along with paintings, literary fiction, and travel accounts, and distilled from those materials a portrayal of Orientalists as people who knowingly or unknowingly abetted and justified the extension of European imperialism through their characterization of "Orientals" as the West's "other": effete, pusillanimous "natives," mired in a static and fatalistic religion whose greatness had irretrievably vanished many centuries ago.

A historian or political scientist bent on advancing this thesis would probably have taken pains to interview some prominent Orientalists before categorically charging them with such profound, if often unconscious, bias; but a methodological conviction that literary or artistic products speak for themselves without additional need to interrogate their creators was commonplace in Said's field of literature. At least that is my conjecture based on what appeared to me to be a distinct disinclination on Said's part, at least up to the 1990s, to interact intellectually or socially with the Columbia faculty charged with teaching about Islam and the Middle East.

This could be too broad a generalization since I may have been unaware of serious conversations between Said and faculty members other than myself. But speaking for myself only, I can remember no more than a dozen brief conversations I had with Edward over the seventeen years we overlapped as faculty members. This despite our living in the same building for eleven years, the last five in the apartment directly above his. (I am omitting conversations relating to his complaints that our young son made too much noise running down the hallway.) More importantly, inasmuch as I directed the Middle East Institute continuously, with but one three-year hiatus, from 1984 to 2000, I was the most visible and most widely published Orientalist then on the faculty. I cannot discount the possibility that my own social inhibitions may have contributed to this lack of contact, but the conversations that we did have suggest to me that Edward had no desire to interact socially with people whom he had charged categorically with harboring hostile and derisive attitudes toward Arabs.

My personal reaction to the publication of *Orientalism* ranged from an overall feeling that Said's jeremiad was too all-encompassing, amounting to throwing out the baby with the bathwater, to a sense of excitement that someone was shaking up a stagnant academic discipline that was particularly weak in historical method and diversity of opinion. Edward once asked me why people in my field, as opposed to his own, so seldom criticized one another's books. I replied that the field was so small and personal relations so important that one risked one's career by criticizing an established scholar. As evidence I cited a letter the Harvard luminary H. A. R. Gibb had written to W. Montgomery Watt at the University of Edinburgh apologizing for a former student of his having had the temerity to write a harsh review of one of Watt's books. (I ran into the letter when I was asked, as the junior faculty factotum at Harvard's Center for Middle East Studies, to clean out Gibb's desk after a stroke forced him into retirement. I also smoked his last cigar and stole his excellent umbrella.) No one can question the fact that Said triggered a wave of criticism by established scholars that continues to some degree to the present day, and I, for one, applaud his boldness in this respect.

However, only in retrospect can I now see two larger aspects of Said's role at Columbia: first, his failure to understand the fledgling field of American Middle East Studies as it had been developing since the 1950s; and second, his basic assumption that thought was more important to scholarship than philology.

A short time prior to a much anticipated debate between Said and Princeton's Bernard Lewis that was to highlight the twentieth annual meeting of the Middle East Studies Association (MESA) in 1980, Edward stopped me on the street and asked me, as the past Executive Secretary of MESA, whether it was not indeed the case that he would be walking into an auditorium filled with ardent disciples of Lewis, whom he had never met. I told him that aside from a small claque of Lewis students and admirers, he would in fact win the debate simply by showing up since most of the MESA membership considered *Orientalism* a masterwork.

Anti-colonialism was then a hallmark of American teaching about the Middle East, and the heavy hand of European imperialism – the Sykes-Picot treaty, British equivocations over Palestine, Russian-British partition of Iran into zones of influence, oppressive French rule in North Africa, and so forth – was drummed into students' heads. By contrast, America's role in the region, a still inchoate project in which many MA students hoped to make their careers, was visualized as not only non-imperialist, but designed to further the emergence of democracy and free enterprise and stifle the advance of communism.

Why Edward did not already know this puzzled me. I subsequently realized, however, that since he had written about the migration of a number of European scholars of Islam to the United States both before and after World War II, and had deduced from this that Americans studying Islam and the Middle East were necessarily steeping in the thought of these English, French, and German role models, therefore an audience of American students of the Middle Eass would by definition be slavish followers of Lewis. In other words, Said fell into a trap that entices all scholars: he believed what he had written.

If he had communicated with the many young Americans in MESA who had been drawn into the field of Middle East Studies because it seemed to be a national priority, he would have discovered that very few of them shared the Europeans' dedication to language mastery and philology, and even fewer were deeply read in the classics of European Orientalism. Gibb at Harvard, Schacht at Columbia, and Gustave E. Von Grunebaum at UCLA each nurtured a handful of doctoral students, but most American students were enrolled in MA programs that gave them very little exposure to the big name Orientalist on their campus. Middle East Studies MA programs then required two years of Classical Arabic (more rarely Turkish or Persian) in addition to a scattering of courses on history, political science, anthropology, religion, and economics, almost all of them taught by professors with weak credentials as Orientalists. Equipped with a hodge-podge of so-called "interdisciplinary" knowledge, and generally a poor grounding in Arabic, the MA recipients moved into positions in government, business, diplomacy, military service, etc.

These graduates would, in the course of their careers, contribute at various levels to American policies and programs aimed at the Middle East, but very few of them thought of the Arab (or the Turk, or the Persian) as a troglodyte "other" suitable only for colonial exploitation. American students grew up with their own "others" in black, Native American, or immigrant communities – in my Midwest hometown the black and Italian communities filled the bill – and knew virtually nothing about Arabs or Muslims, and even less about Turks and Persians. American Middle East studies, in other words, was its own thing; it bore little relationship to European oriental studies.

This does not mean that it was better, of course. Mediocre training and deeply flawed insights into the targeted societies and cultures dogged the Middle East regional studies programs until they fell into disrepute toward the end of the twentieth century. But those weaknesses differed from the ones Said was charging the Orientalists with. The dominant paradigm of the 1960s, modernization theory, did not demean the "orientals" and doom them to serving colonial masters. Instead, it maintained that every society in the world – except those deceived by communism and socialism – would ultimately make it to the Promised Land of the modern industrial world. They just had to follow the American example. The job of the area specialist was to identify and encourage the "change agents" or "men on the move" who would lead their people into that bright future. The final idiocy of this theory took the form of "nation building" during the presidency of George W. Bush, but "modernization" and "nation building" did not correspond to Said's characterization of Orientalism.

In the 1960s and 1970s a handful of social scientists, none of them steeped in the European orientalist tradition, articulated versions of modernization theory that would apply to the Middle East. If one reads the books of this group of professors, one discovers that they tend to acknowledge one another in their prefaces, often as members of the same committees, such as the Joint Committee on the Near and Middle East of the Social Science Research Council and American Council of Learned Societies. Names that come to mind are J. C. Hurewitz (Columbia), Charles Issawi (Columbia-Princeton), Manfred Halpern and Morroe Berger (Princeton), Dankwart Rustow (Princeton-Columbia-CUNY), Daniel Bell (MIT), Nadav Safran (Harvard), Leonard Binder (Chicago), Malcolm Kerr (UCLA), and John C. Campbell (Department of State). Bernard Lewis, who migrated from the School of Oriental and African Studies of the University of London to Princeton in 1974, was singular in being superbly educated in European Orientalism and also contributing a path-breaking book that explicitly combined Orientalism and modernization, *The Emergence of Modern Turkey* (1961).

If Said had found his Columbia colleague Jay Hurewitz's company tolerable, he might have developed a deeper insight into the American way of studying the Middle East. But he was suspicious. He once asked me how extensive Hurewitz's influence was at Columbia. He was surprised, I think, when I told him that Hurewitz had wielded the meager financial and administrative tools at his disposal as Director of the Middle East Institute before 1984 in such a way as to alienate pretty much every professor in MELAC ... and me as well. To Edward's way of thinking, Jay should have been a dominant Orientalist presence on the faculty, but like the other influential social scientists of that generation, Hurewitz came from a World War II and postwar diplomatic/intelligence background rather than a European Orientalist program. He was neither a philologist, nor a student of Semitic religion, nor deeply knowledgeable about classical Islamic matters.

Hurewitz was, however, the first Jew to head a major Middle East program, a fact that he was acutely aware of. Perhaps because of this, he minimized his Jewish roots – his father was a rabbi – even to the extent of holding class on high holy days. Oddly enough, the one thing Edward and Jay had in common was a consuming interest in Palestine, the former as an advocate for his fellow Palestinians and the latter as the determinedly (if sometimes self-deceived) neutral – à la the US State Department – author of a widely read history entitled *The Struggle for Palestine* (1950).

Over the six years or so that I co-taught a seminar with Hurewitz, I developed a good deal of antipathy toward his approach to education. He insisted on using the word "training" to describe what we were doing, and he demanded that the students submit an outline of their seminar projects by the second week of the course, instructing them on the exact form an outline must take. As back-up teacher, I tried to support his program as one that would reliably produce a finished paper by the end of the year, but I would also mention that I myself could never follow such regimentation. I suspect that this lack of harmony is what eventually led Jay to reschedule the class, without consulting me, for a time when I had another teaching commitment.

Said offered a puzzling contrast with Hurewitz's idea of how to train area specialists. On two occasions I served with him on PhD thesis defenses in comparative literature. One of them went badly because of a quarrel between Edward and the dissertation sponsor, Michael Riffaterre. The other mystified me. The thesis was on the literature of partition, a comparison of literature in Ireland and Northern Ireland, on the one hand, and of literature in Israel and among the Palestinians, on the other. It was effectively written and highly intelligent. But the doctoral candidate knew neither Hebrew nor Arabic. During the deliberations at the end of the defense, I remarked that sponsors of history and political science dissertations dealing with the Middle East invariably required some knowledge of the languages relevant to the subject. Was it the case, therefore, that in comparative literature, of all places, knowledge of languages other than English was not required? No one responded. So I voted to pass what was, in intellectual terms, a very good piece of work. But I left the room amazed that Edward, as the sponsor, had not expected more of his student.

As I ruminated over this incident, it gradually dawned on me that European Orientalism, whether pre- or post-Said, has always started with language. A solid command of classical written texts, preferably in more than one Middle Eastern language, has been the sine qua non for acceptance into the Orientalist guild. By contrast, American Middle Eastern studies programs paid lip service to language acquisition, but literary mastery was a rare attainment, particularly from the 1990s onward when speaking surpassed classical reading as the most useful instructional goal. The social scientists who forged the conceptual bases for Middle East studies during the 1960s often had little or no knowledge of a Middle Eastern language, particularly if they were Americans born and educated.

So how can I account for Said's cavalier attitude toward doctoral level studies of his mother tongue? My only answer is that he thought ideas were more important than propaideutic skill acquisition. A "training" regime like Hurewitz's, which was not unlike the classes I took as a student of the Middle East at Harvard, required a modest level of language qualification, but little emphasis was placed on ideas. By contrast, Said saw a student who was intellectually and literarily capable of writing a fine doctoral thesis, despite a lack of the "necessary" languages, and gave him a green light to do so.

Thought has its limits, however. My last firm memory of Said was his attendance in 2000 at a seminar given by the distinguished Arab intellectual Aziz al-Azmeh, who stated firmly, with Edward seemingly in tacit agreement, that nothing had been written by western scholars of Islam and the Arab world since the publication of *Orientalism* that departed in any significant way from Said's depiction of the Orientalist paradigm. Astonished by this statement, I asked al-Azmeh how closely he had followed post-*Orientalism* scholarly writing on Islam and the Middle East. He responded that nothing written since 1978 had been couched in challenging enough prose to be taken seriously. When I followed up with a query as to whether he believed that it was impossible to express important thoughts in simple language, al-Azmeh said that that was exactly what he meant. Anything not marinated in post-colonial cultural theory jargon was not worth reading.

Edward may have remained silent in the debate out of friendship with the speaker or for health reasons, but he must have had mixed feelings about the exchange. On the one hand, al-Azmeh was ascribing to his work an unfathomable profundity; but on the other, he was saying that Said's intervention in the field of Islamic and Middle East studies had changed nothing ... at least in that field. In a more recent personal communication, Salman Sayyid, the Leeds University Professor of Social Theory and Decolonial Thought, has remarked:

> I find it particularly interesting how Orientalism has resonated
> in fields other than Islamic studies and cognate subjects. Perhaps
> one problem with Said's critique is that it was associated with an
> epistemology that emerges from an articulation between the work
> of Foucault and Gramsci. This innovative coupling helped to propel
> Orientalism beyond the confines of Islamic Studies, but also hindered
> its reception in that field, since it hinted at an epistemological stance
> that for the most part was considered to be alien and irrelevant.

For the past thirty years I have lived in the spacious apartment where Edward wrote *Orientalism* and crafted five of my own books in what was once his study. The apartment was a reward for years of service helping to revise Columbia University real estate policies, not for my scholarship. From time to time I think about Edward looking out the window at Morningside Park and seeing the same vista that I see now, and I ponder the impact a scholar's words and ideas may, or may not, have over time.

Marshall, Meet Edward

What can one conjecture about how Said and Hodgson would have interact-
ed had their life paths intersected? To begin with, I can imagine that each of
them would have reacted warmly to the other's critical approach to the cor-
pus of French and English Orientalist works. Despite his silence when Aziz
al-Azmeh declared *Orientalism* to have had no effect on the field of Islamic
studies, Said noted in *Orientalism* that:

> Scholars and critics who are trained in the traditional Orientalist
> disciplines are perfectly capable of freeing themselves from
> the old ideological straitjacket. Jacques Berque's and Maxime
> Rodinson's training ranks with the most rigorous available, but what
> invigorates their investigations even of traditional problems is their
> methodological self-consciousness. For if Orientalism has historically
> been too smug, too insulated, too positivistically confident in its ways
> and its premises, then one way of opening oneself to what one studies
> in or about the Orient is reflexively to submit one's method to critical
> scrutiny. This is what characterizes Berque and Rodinson, each in his
> own way. What one finds in their work is always, first of all, a direct
> sensitivity to the material before them, and then a continual self-
> examination of their methodology and practice, a constant attempt
> to keep their work responsive to the material and not to a doctrinal
> preconception. [pp. 326–7]

I can't imagine a better description of what Marshall Hodgson attempted
in *The Venture of Islam*, a work that truly delivers a "continual self-examina-
tion of ... methodology and practice." Said was not interested in Americans,
however. With respect to the "good" Orientalists that he names, I can see his
point with Jacques Berque better than with Maxime Rodinson. Rodinson, a
French professor of classical Ethiopian who was also knowledgeable in Arabic and Hebrew, wrote on many subjects.

Rodinson's sociologically informed *Mohammed* (1974) became his most
widely read book in English and a frequently assigned classroom text. The
Freudian psychologizing he brought, in my view ineffectively, to the biog-
raphy of the Prophet was certainly methodologically self-conscious, but
enough Muslim readers found his approach disrespectful of Islam to get it
banned from the American University in Cairo in 1999.

It is likely that the Rodinson work that attracted Said's attention was
not *Mohammed*, but *Israel: A Colonial Settler State?* This was a 1974 translation
of an essay originally published in 1967 in a special issue of *Les Temps mod-
ernes* devoted to the Six-Day War. Rodinson was a politically engaged scholar

and one of the few classical Orientalists who continued to provide advice to the French foreign ministry in the 1980s.

His considered view of Said, which Hodgson is likely to have agreed with, was expressed as qualified praise in his 1988 book *Europe and the Mystique of Islam*:

> Edward Said's *Orientalism* had a great and unexpected success. There are many valuable ideas in it. Its great merit, to my mind, was to shake the self-satisfaction of many Orientalists, to appeal to them (with questionable success) to consider the sources and the connections of their ideas, to cease to see them as a natural, unprejudiced conclusion of the facts, studied without any presupposition. But, as usual, his militant stand leads him repeatedly to make excessive statements. This problem is accentuated because as a specialist of English and comparative literature, he is inadequately versed in the practical work of the Orientalists. It is too easy to choose, as he does, only English and French Orientalists as a target. By doing so, he takes aim only at representatives of huge colonial empires. But there was an Orientalism before the empires, and the pioneers of Orientalism were often subjects of other European countries, some without colonies. Much too often, Said falls into the same traps that we old Communist intellectuals fell into some forty years ago.... The growth of Orientalism was linked to the colonial expansion of Europe in a much more subtle and intrinsic way than he imagines. Moreover, his nationalistic tendencies have prevented him from considering, among others, the studies of Chinese or Indian civilizations, which are ordinarily regarded as part of the field of Orientalism. For him, the Orient is restricted to *his* East, that is, the Middle East. Muslim countries outside the Arab world (after all, four Muslims in five are not Arabs), and even Arab nations in the West receive less than their due in his interpretation.

This reflective view does not appear in the French version of the book published in 1980 – before Said's work had become well known – as *La Fascination de l'Islam*. In the Introduction to this work devoted to unstinting admiration of the European Orientalist tradition, Rodinson wrote: "Le danger seulement serait qu'en poussant à la limite certaines analyses et, encore plus, certaines formulations d'Edward Said, on tombe dans une doctrine toute semblable à la théorie jdanovienne des deux sciences." [p.14] The reference here is to Stalin's rigid ideology chief Andrei Zhdanov, who insisted on the pseudo-scientific development theory of Lysenkoism and disciplined Eurocommunists who did not toe the Stalinist line. Rodinson deleted this negative comment, which expressed a feeling that Said's ideas were too rigidly doctrinaire, from the English translation of his book. I once asked him during an airplane flight to a conference why he did this. He gave a Gallic shrug and said: "I didn't know then that Said was important."

The softening of Rodinson's opinion echoes his statement that Said's book met *unexpected* success. Who would have thought that an English professor would author a transformative work on Islam and the Middle East? A common criticism raised by Said's critics well into the 1980s, which Hodgson might or might not have concurred in, was that he believed – or better, some of his most avid readers believed – that everyone brought up in an imperialist country was so imbued with pejorative attitudes toward "the other" that even good will could not prevent them from tainting an individual's work.

This is all surmise, of course. If Hodgson and Said ever had met in person, I'm sure they would not have discussed Orientalism. Said did not converse with Orientalists.

Orientalism since 9/11

When I started studying medieval Islam, I understood the Orientalist viewpoint as arising out of Classical and Biblical studies and as being deeply informed by seeing Islam in comparison with Christianity and Judaism, and the Middle East and North Africa in comparison with Europe. Other parts of the world, such as East Asia and South Asia, were historiographical domains unto themselves. Now, sixty years later, broad-spectrum discussions of world or interregional history usually compare Europe with China, and sometimes with India. Despite Hodgson's attempt to promote Islam as a world civilization arising in the Middle East, medieval Islamic history has become a historiographical domain – if not a backwater – unto itself, particularly if one detaches religious studies from history writ large. What this amounts to is a provincialization, and more recently an intense politicization, of Islamic history. Not only is its relevance to other historical fields less apparent than it seemed to be in 1960, but the debate over Saidian "Orientalism" has cast a by now tedious shadow over the achievements of everyone who worked in the European tradition from 1800 to 1978.

The current convergence of European, East Asian, and South Asian history derives in large part from the study of parallel developments of social and especially economic history in those regions. Sadly, the absence of similar efforts devoted to the Middle East and North Africa has diminished their salience to broad discussions of world history.

Compounding this neglect of social and economic history, and the continuing preference advocated by Hodgson for scrutinizing literary high culture within the Islamic world, is the baleful impact of contemporary politics. Because the events of 9/11 introduced Americans and Europeans to a type of violence they had never thought would affect them, and because the perpetrators and apologists for that violence choose to invoke Islam in explaining their actions, a powerful pressure has developed to "understand" Islam as a political force whose contemporary manifestations have medieval roots. Though this viewpoint consciously affects only a portion of the scholarly work undertaken in this century, it has had a broader effect in reinforcing a way of seeing the world, both present and past, through Islam-colored glasses. As a social and economic historian I find this tendency deplorable and take note of the fact that studies of other world areas, notably China, India, and Japan, are comparatively unburdened by religious/ideological presumptions and fears.

I was eighteen in 1959 when I first took a class on Islam at Harvard. It was called Islamic Institutions and was taught by Robert Bellah, who went on to become a major figure in the sociology of religion, though to the best of my knowledge, he never wrote extensively on Islam. By the time I began publishing my own work in the early 1970s, I was convinced that given the obvious and manifold weaknesses in the Orientalist scholarship – overwhelmingly European – devoted to Islamic studies, my generation could not help but make major advances at both the empirical and the conceptual level. My first exposure, at a conference at St. Antony's College, Oxford in 1967, to the doyens of medieval Islamic history – Claude Cahen, Samuel Stern, Richard Walzer, S. D. Goitein, Dominique Sourdel, and others – reinforced my sense that European Orientalism was a small and elite club that had little or no use for fledgling Americans. In the absence of a mentor who might have sponsored me for membership in that club, I persisted in going my own way.

I am now seventy-six, and the major advances that I foresaw as the destiny of my generation never came to pass, or perhaps were preempted by the thoughts of Hodgson and Said. To be sure, a great deal of scholarship was published during the intervening years; but for the most part, I have not seen it as presenting a superior paradigm or template for understanding Islam or the various societies shaped by Islam. Skills at reading, critiquing, and challenging high literary texts have doubtless improved, particularly with regard to the first three Islamic centuries; but as productive as this trend has been, it has served to reinforce a tradition that ascribes everything of interest in Islam, both as a religion and as a focus of history, to that early period. Sadly, the period from 1000 to 1300, continues to be understudied and dismissed as of lesser importance, despite Hodgson's recognition of it as a crucial era.

A steadily growing appreciation of *The Venture of Islam* has worked against this tendency to some degree. But its lack of a feeling for social and economic history limits its value for assessing the broad structuring trends in Islamic history.

Where will, or should, Islamic studies go from here? As a scholar entering upon retirement, my own part in that future will be minimal. Moreover, the transformation – one can almost say metastasis – of an essentialized "Islam" in the minds of many Europeans and Americans since 9/11 has cast a pall over the entire field. Books written to challenge, reform, defend, deride, or apologize for Islam far outnumber those devoted to a less engaged scholarship. This is not to say that engagement is bad; but it tends, sometimes quite subtly, to shape a writer's project even when the project is focused on the pre-Mongol period. (Who cared about Ibn Taimiyya in 1950?)

Since Hodgson died before Edward Said's *Orientalism* was published, there is no easy way to put them in dialogue with each other. But Said himself died in 2003, only five months after President George W. Bush celebrated "mission accomplished" in Iraq. Thus Said's famous intervention in the field of Islamic studies was made long before the attacks of 9/11, and the American and European responses to those attacks. For Hodgson, Orientalism was what several generations of European scholars interested intellectually in Islam and the Middle East engaged in without recognizing certain rigidities in their own presuppositions. For Said Orientalism was worse than that: a pathology that distorted the thoughts and writings of those same Europeans, including some who had migrated to the United States. Imperialism was the root of that pathology, and implicit or explicit racism its technique.

Today, however, when Islam has unexpectedly resurfaced as a topic of both popular and specialized interest, the trope of imperialist enablement has become less salient than an openly expressed fear and hatred of Muslims. The Orientalists of yesteryear, whether of Hodgsonian or Saidian description, have been joined by, or sometimes keep company with, thinkers who are consumed with a new mindset, that of Islamophobia.

Whatever Said's intentions in writing *Orientalism*, the broad acceptance of his description of European and American scholars of Islam and the Middle East as disseminators of distorted, stereotyped, and ill-informed opinions has resulted in tagging these scholars as conscious or unconscious agents of imperialism. But Said did not contend with out-and-out Islamophobia. No one can question the utility of his analysis as a basis for a critical appraisal of scholarship or its value in sparking salutary self-criticism within the targeted scholarly community. But with the attacks of 9/11 touching off a crisis of formerly unimaginable magnitude, how is a scholar with years of contemplation of Islamic history under his belt – fifty years in my own case – to comport himself? Possibilities arise that earlier generations would not have considered.

One might decide that the sins of past and present Orientalists make it imperative to withhold public expression of one's scholarly opinion lest one contribute to fresh imperialist evils. I have heard well-informed colleagues refuse to respond to questions inspired by governmental policy considerations for just this reason. They did not want to be tarred with the stigma of collaboration. But this option leaves an open field for the Islamophobes.

One might offer one's opinions provisionally but emphasize that scholars working within, or with at least ancestral connection to, the cultural traditions in question should be considered a priori to have superior knowledge and insight deriving from their post-colonial status. But should one then suggest which post-colonial voices to prefer as the most valuable? And which to shun?

One might take the presumptively counter-Orientalist position of assuming that all acts of United States governments past, present, and future deserve denunciation as imperialist endeavors. Again, this cedes the function of assessing current government policy options to the Islamophobes.

Or one might speak as a private citizen about non-Islam-related domestic matters but recuse oneself from venturing into more problematic areas on the grounds that the knowledge one has acquired in one's career is worse than worthless.

The way I have worded these alternatives has probably signaled my disinclination to follow any of them. As an adoptive New Yorker who could see from his apartment window the plume of smoke from the World Trade Center, I simply cannot accept the Saidian proposition that my life's work, if brought to bear on our contemporary tragedy, will do more harm than good because as a successor to the Orientalists of old I have acquired imperialist predilections simply by growing up in an imperialist society without benefit of ancestral roots in the Arab or Muslim worlds. I also find it hard to credit that the many people who subscribe to Said's viewpoint would prefer to have public discourse and government policy informed by people who have never studied the Arab or Muslim worlds, or, worse, have studied them from a starting point of visceral hatred. Is ignorance, I would ask them, better than Orientalism?

The question might be avoided by saying that the news media and policy makers should turn at this juncture exclusively to Muslim analysts living in the societies where animosity toward the United States is most intense, or at least to people with roots in those societies living in the United States or in Europe. Such scholars have wisely been sought out, to be sure, and some have courted denunciation by their fellows by not offering blanket condemnations of US policies. But it is obvious that scholars who do not have the proper ethnic or religious pedigree have been and will continue to be consulted as well.

Thus we come to a scholarly impasse. The post-9/11 years have seen an intensified interest in Islam, Islamic history, the Muslim cultures of Asia and Africa, and the adaptation of Muslim immigrants to life in predominantly non-Muslim societies. They have also seen the firm and overdue, but by no means unchallenged, absorption of American Muslims into our national life. Whose ideas are shaping this intellectual enterprise?

In my judgment, events have conspired to uncover the barrenness of the most negative interpretation of Said's Orientalist hypothesis. I have no problem finding fault with particular ideas espoused by Orientalists past and present, but the proposition that westerners studying the non-west inevitably and irretrievably lead nations and governments astray points to a policy of preferring ignorance to knowledge and preferring guidance from abroad to guidance from within one's own society.

What is wanted is a top-to-bottom reconsideration of how we arrived at the historic moment we are living through, a reconsideration that reaches beyond the question of whether the United States should or should not endorse Palestinian statehood, beyond the question of whether American forces should or should not have set boots on Arab or Afghan soil, beyond the question of whether Cold War calculations should or should not have prompted the United States to support Afghan groups whose religious ideologies it was unwilling to sanction, beyond the question of how the United States may have been involved in the failure of the Arab Spring. All of these questions are worth investigating, but they point to an underlying presumption that the roots of our current crises are chronologically recent and firmly anchored in the District of Columbia.

There are other, harder questions that require deeper and more far-ranging analysis. Why did most of the independent governments of the Muslim world adopt an attitude of hostility toward Islamic religious institutions and scholars from the early nineteenth century onward? As for the European states that today see so clearly the defects of American foreign policy, what role did they play during the colonial era in fostering religious divisiveness in the Muslim world? Why did secular nationalism give rise to police-state government in much of the Islamic world, and why have Western governments regarded such governments as progressive? Have several decades of Western scholarly assault on the fundamentals of Islamic belief – the historicity of Muhammad and the Qur'an, the genuineness of the traditions of the Prophet, the reliability of the Islamic historical tradition – played a significant role in intensifying friction with Muslims?

Questions like these, which I believe can only be addressed by historians with Orientalist skills, can help guide efforts to rethink the history of contacts between Muslims and non-Muslims from the seventh century onward. What will come of these efforts cannot be known in detail, but historians will probably discern a deep Christian animosity toward Islam dating back to the seventh century, when most of the world's Christians suddenly came under the rule of Arab Muslims. No one denies this animosity during the medieval and early modern periods, punctuated as they were by the crusades and innumerable wars with the Ottoman Empire. But the continuation of this animosity during the succeeding period of European ascendancy was cloaked by imperialist rhetoric, paeans for Westernization, and the nurture of proxy "modernizing" governments willing to suppress Islam in return for Western favor.

Many episodes in this centuries-long confrontation with Islam are well known, but they have not been engrossed into the sort of broad structural synthesis that can incorporate contemporary events. Lacking such a synthesis, the quest for causes reaches back only a few decades and misses the intimate relationship between western policies toward the Muslim world and the policies of nominally Muslim governments toward their own citizenry. Without a clear understanding of that relationship, attempts to address the sources of discord will surely fall short of success.

In this sort of endeavor, I believe that despite its limitations, Hodgson's breadth of vision provides more scope for rethinking the history of Islam and its role in world affairs than does Said's diatribe. But Said's critical eye penetrated more deeply into the conscious and unconscious complications that might be involved in such rethinking.

A Big Bang, Big Crunch Theory of Islamic History
(2010)

THE ANALOGY WITH COSMOLOGY embodied in this title represents an effort to identify a distinctive and recurrent pattern in Islamic religious history: a "big bang" is a religious singularity, that is to say, a homogeneous consensus on what constitutes the universe of all possible expressions of Islam. From this point of homogeneity the Muslim umma "expands" or diverges rapidly and becomes highly heterogeneous. Then the expansion slows. The community begins to contract as if being drawn toward a new singularity by the force of gravity. This is the "big crunch" hypothesized by cosmologists. It results in a new singularity that differs from the first one but shares a high degree of homogeneity. Then the process starts anew with a fresh process of expansion.

This conjectural cycle has recurred three times in Islamic history, and we are currently in the midst of a fourth cycle. The Qur'an itself, God's unchanging word revealed through Muhammad, was the first singularity. It encompassed all possible Islams. The expansion phase took the form of a vast proliferation and broad geographical distribution of hadith, reports of what Muhammad and some of his earliest companions said or did as they strove to lead their lives in accordance with the Qur'an. In principle, any person who had direct exposure to the Prophet could be the author of a hadith.[1] Consequently, the number of reports that found their way into circulation numbered in the hundreds of thousands. The contraction phase of this first big bang cycle began with the systematic quest on the part of hadith specialists for "sound" hadith, that is to say, hadith that had a high probability of being historically veracious. Given an unwillingness to accept a specialist's personal opinion about the substance to any hadith, the winnowing process, which involved the rejection of tens of thousands of reports that some Muslims believed to be true, focused on examining the chain of oral communication that tied the text to the Prophet. It was reasoned that while this might lead to true hadith being overlooked, a sound chain of transmission provided the best evidence of a sound text. This process culmi-

---

1. For details concerning the eligibility of hadith authors see Miklós Murányi, *Die Prophetengenossen in der frühislamischen Geschichte*. Dissertation, Orientalischer Seminar der Universität Bonn, Bonn 1973, In: *Bonner Orientalische Studien*, Bd. 28.

nated in the collection of six Sunni hadith collections and four Shi'ite ones. Over the course of several centuries, these books became canonical for each of those branches of the Muslim community. This canonization formed the second singularity. Thenceforward, Qur'an plus Sunna, that is, the collective instructions imparted by canonical hadith, would encompass all conceivable Islams.

The second cycle began chronologically as the "sound" hadith collections were being compiled but before they became canonical. Hence this cycle overlaps the first one, which is okay since we are dealing here with pure conjecture. The focus of the second cycle was law. On the basis of Qur'an, Sunna, reasoning by analogy, and scholarly consensus, a wide variety of hotly competing Sunni legal schools (*madhhabs*) arose. Shi'ism and Ibadi *kharijism* developed separate legal schools. The expansion phase of this cycle involved intense animosities amounting, in some Iranian cities, to mini-civil wars. Though the legal rubrics used to label these animosities may conceal other social divisions (for example, ethnicity, class, priority of conversion to Islam), issues relating specifically to legal requirements, reasoning, or monopolization of judicial roles cannot be discounted. The contraction phase saw most of the legal schools dying out and the eventual emergence by the fourteenth century of a consensus in the mutual recognition of four Sunni schools: Hanafi, Shafi'i, Maliki, and Hanbali, along with the Shi'ite and Ibadi alternatives. The new singularity that resulted from the big crunch of the second cycle consisted of Qur'an, Sunna, and Shari'a. Thenceforward these encompassed the totality of conceivable Islams. Modern books offering comprehensive descriptions of the faith almost invariably describe Sunni legal differences in terms of mutual acceptance and regional variation and ignore the period of bitter and sometimes lethal rivalry among them that was still in evidence five hundred years after Muhammad's death.

The second cycle also reflects the geographical evolution of the Muslim umma. The first cycle had focused on hadith, which by definition gave primacy to locations to which Muhammad's early followers had dispersed and related stories of his words and deeds. Scholars in search of sound hadith traveled more often to Mecca, Medina, Basra, Kufa, and Baghdad than to locales in, say, Egypt or Spain. Yet the collections that eventually became canonical were conceived of as reflecting all of Islam despite the fact that the collectors happened all to be Iranian.

The strong animosities that characterized the second cycle corresponded to the development of increasingly regionalized homogeneities in how people lived their faith. As the umma expanded through conversion, the centripetal attraction of the cities that had earlier drawn legions of itinerant

hadith collectors was overtaken by regional identities shaped by local con-
stellations of Muslim scholars. The big crunch of the second cycle, therefore,
represented the solidification of a particular law school's dominance in a
city or region more often than it did a resolution of the specific legal differences between schools. Where the first big crunch represented agreement
on the empirical bases of the Sunna, the second was more an agreement to
disagree peaceably on matters of legal contention.

The third cycle began as the second was in its contraction phase. It
manifested itself in the form of organized Sufism. Elevated forms of super-
erogatory religious devotion had attracted individual Muslims from the
earliest days of the umma. Admiration for outstanding practitioners of separate trends in asceticism, pietism, and mysticism inspired the collection
of bits of poetry attributed to them and reports of their ecstatic utterances
and activities. Not until the eleventh century, however, did followers of one
or another exemplary pious individual organize themselves into fraternal
groups. These groups typically combined ascetic, pietistic, and mystic practices and sometimes added in other group activities such as singing, dancing,
and young men's athletic-cum-militia exercises (*futuwwa*).

Massive expansion over an enormous geographical area resulted in hundreds, if not thousands, of Sufi brotherhoods (*tariqa*, pl. *turuq*) being formed.
Sunni communities were more strongly affected than Shi'ite ones, possibly
because the Muharram ceremonies commemorating the martyrdom of the
third Imam, al-Husain b. Ali, offered mass emotional catharsis that competed with Sufi rituals. Unlike hadith collecting or legal disputation, belonging
to a Sufi brotherhood did not require literacy or education. Thus the third
cycle corresponds to the full penetration of Islam into all ranks and levels of
society, and the Sufi brotherhoods provided venues for accommodating local pre-Islamic religious attitudes and practices that the Muslim community
encountered as it expanded increasingly into Asia and Africa after 1300, a
date that roughly corresponds to the spread of the first brotherhoods. The
brotherhoods also elevated group membership and devotion to a local saintly individual (variously termed a *shaikh*, a *pir*, a *murshid*, a *marabout*, etc.) to
a level that competed with or surpassed attachment to a generalized Sunna
or a school of legal thought. (One might compare this with the myriad of
Protestant denominations succeeding or coexisting with earlier notions of a
universal Catholic church.)

At a certain point, a new contraction began. Influential Muslim leaders, most often legal scholars but including modernizers and secularists,
identified some brotherhoods as too obscurantist, too superstitious, or too
syncretistic in incorporating non-Muslim traditions. Certain governments,

notably Egypt and the Ottoman Empire in the nineteenth century, moved against selected Sufi brotherhoods in order to suppress loyalties to non-government authorities, namely, the Sufi *shaikhs*, and to prevent subjects from devoting themselves to transregional organizations. During the contraction phase, most Sufi brotherhoods disappeared, but some survived by adapting to changing circumstances or by spearheading anti-colonial movements in Sudan, Morocco, Algeria, Afghanistan, and elsewhere.

Specific instances of brotherhood survival aside, the basic principle of organized piety embodied in the concept of a *tariqa*, which connoted formal membership in an organization and oaths of loyalty to the organization's leader, survived the third big crunch. The twentieth century saw the formation of organizations like the Muslim Brotherhood that retained the structure of a Sufi *tariqa*, including devotion to a brotherhood leader, but discarded the mystic or superstitious elements that clashed with increasingly modern religious attitudes. This yielded a fresh singularity consisting of Qur'an, Sunna, Shari'a, and Tariqa, meaning sworn membership in a specific religious association. (The final term in this formulation includes both other-worldly and this-worldly pietistic membership organizations, including revival [*da'wa*] groups and religious political parties).

The fourth cycle has followed the pattern of the first three by overlapping in time the contraction of its predecessor, the brotherhood cycle. It began with the advent of Islamic modernism triggered by contact with Western culture and access to new modes of disseminating ideas: the printing press (late nineteenth century and often lithographic for most religious publications from Morocco to Indonesia) followed by audio, video, and electronic media. With Sufism largely passing away, this new expansion of Islam featured a wide spectrum of "new" ideas about Islam, many, if not most, propounded by men, and occasionally women, who were/are not of the ulama, and who were/are often self-educated or minimally educated in traditional religious matters. This cycle has made possible sudden enthusiasms for innovative ideas that run the gamut from nihilism, to revolutionary violence, to secularizing reform; it also provides tools for reasserting traditional commitments of different aspects of Sunna and Shari'a. I believe we are currently reaching the maximum expansion of this cycle and are witnessing the beginning of a new contraction phase. The current struggles among secularists, moderate reformers, Islamic State and al-Qaeda devotees, Salafists, and Muslim political parties are characteristic of the late phase of a big bang-big crunch cycle.

Much more might be said about each of the cycles, but taken together they suggest three lessons that are of importance to Islam today. First, the

Muslim umma seems to possess a "gravitational" force that keeps it from diverging indefinitely and draws it back to a new center once a cycle of expansion has reached some limit. This sets Islam apart from the comparable world faith communities of Buddhism and Christianity, which have progressively subdivided over time with very little recentering.

Second, while ritual invocations of geographical centrality in the form of prayer orientation toward the Kaaba (*qibla*) and performance of the *hajj* and *'umra* pilgrimages to Mecca undoubtedly reinforce the idea that all Muslims share common roots, the contraction phase of each cycle has seen dedicated religious specialists playing a central role in establishing limits to expansion without resorting to anathematization of their brethren. This betokens an underlying conviction that disagreements within Islam are best dealt with diplomatically.

Third, each new "singularity" has incorporated and sanctified some degree of diversity – six canonical hadith collections, four law schools, a number of "moderate" neo-Sufi or Sufi-like organizations – as reflecting a broad variety of organized pious observance.

Looking at the current cycle from this perspective, one might hazard some conjectures about the future: 1) Most of the new ideas about Islam propounded over the past century will not survive a new contraction ... but some will. 2) Those that do survive will converge on some new principle(s) that will contribute to a new singularity. Possibilities that come to mind include a) acceptance of lay thinkers as legitimate interpreters of Islam, b) acceptance of the idea of "national" ummas contained within the boundaries of nation-states, c) acceptance of new interpretations that converge with the moral desiderata of so-called Western culture, d) declaration that certain parts of the Muslim past, for example, slavery or capital punishment for apostasy, no longer have validity. 3) Highly educated, professional scholars of religion will play a key, though not necessarily exclusive, role in prompting and directing the coming big crunch.

Abu Muslim and Charlemagne
(2009)

"WITHOUT ISLAM, the Frankish Empire would have probably never existed, and Charlemagne, without Muhammad, would be inconceivable."

This idea [today I would term it a conjecture] encapsulating the central thesis of Henri Pirenne's 1937 classic *Mohammed and Charlemagne*[1] did not excite universal agreement, but it sparked questions and counter-theses that greatly advanced historical studies of the Mediterranean in medieval times. Textual researchers and archaeologists asked what products were traded across the sea? At what dates? In what quantities? What impact did the shrinkage of trade have? Did the expansion of Islam terminate an antecedent unity among the littoral lands? Or did the Roman era unity vanish long before Muhammad?

Without rehearsing the decades-long debate over the Pirenne thesis, it can nevertheless be observed that the economic history of Iran played little role in it. The thesis raised questions specifically related to the Mediterranean basin, mostly in its western portion. Events on the high plateau of Iran beyond the Zagros Mountains, which make up Iran's frontier with Iraq, were seen as too remote to be relevant. Scholars interested in flows of precious metal, whether coined or uncoined, sometimes provided exceptions to this rule. Notably, Sture Bolin's 1952 article, "Mohammed, Charlemagne and Ruric,"[2] sought to account for the vast hordes of Iranian silver coins found in Sweden and northeast Europe.

The conjecture that will be advanced in the following pages is that developments in Iran proper had a profound effect on the Mediterranean zone, in both its eastern and its western portions. When in 750 the Iranian insurrectionary Abu Muslim led a movement from the east to topple the Umayyad caliphate and put in its place the descendants of Muhammad's uncle, al-Abbas, the outcome was not just a transfer of the caliphal capital from Damascus to the soon-to-be-built Abbasid capital of Baghdad. It marked the beginning of an Iranian political and economic dominance that lasted until the eleventh century, at which time a climate shift to colder winters in Siberia brought about a severe decline in agricultural production in northern

---

1. *Mahomet et Charlemagne* (Paris, 1937), translated as *Mohammed and Charlemagne*, B. Miall (London, 1956).

2. *Scandinavian Economic History Review* 1 (1952): 5–39.

Iran, northern Mesopotamia, and eastern Anatolia. This climatic deterioration, which began in the first decade of the eleventh century and lasted for over a century, led eventually to a reorientation of the Muslim heartland back toward the Mediterranean. Great Iranian cities like Nishapur, Rayy, Herat, and Isfahan fell into decline while Arab cities like Cairo, Damascus, Aleppo, and Tunis gained unprecedented prominence.

With respect to the western Mediterranean, and al-Andalus in particular, the question that will be asked is whether the downgrading of caliphal relations with the west in favor of the east for some three and a half centuries, from roughly 775 to 1125, contributed significantly to the distinctive social, religious, and intercommunal relations in al-Andalus that we today call convivencia, as well as to the rise of Charlemagne's Frankish empire. Or is convivencia in al-Andalus simply the best-studied example of an intercommunal modus vivendi that was characteristic of medieval Islam in general?

Basic political facts are not open to question:

1) After ca. 740 when the Syrian army sent to northwest Africa to suppress a rebellion by the indigenous population suffered defeat and retreated into Spain, the territories we now think of as Morocco and Algeria lost political contact with the caliphate. Precise details cannot always be relied on because the extant narratives of early Islamic times in North Africa come from centuries later and contain a good deal of fanciful material. It appears, however, that local regimes or movements embodying Alid, kharijite, or homegrown Berber ideas came quickly to dominate the great swath of territory between the Tunisian coastal lowlands and the Atlantic Ocean.

2) In 800 the Abbasid caliph Harun al-Rashid granted the governorship of Tunisia and Tripolitania to the Aghlabid family on a hereditary basis. The Aghlabids continued to recognize Abbasid sovereignty and to send annual fixed tribute payments. But little or nothing flowed in the opposite direction in terms of military or political reinforcement.

3) After the Abbasid defeat of the Umayyads in 750, Syria fell into a state of petty tribal altercations that lasted until the time of the first crusade at the end of the eleventh century.

4) The Fatimid dynasty that arose in Tunisia in 909, took over Egypt in 969, and proceeded on to occupy a good part of Palestine never provoked a significant military response from the Abbasids. This would be hard to explain if the territories gobbled up in the Fatimid

expansion had been core contributors to the caliphate's military and economic might, as were the various regions of Iran where local rebellions repeatedly prompted strong caliphal reactions down until 945, when the Iranian Buyid warlords gained control of Baghdad and of the person of the caliph.

Reinforcing this image of a Muslim empire whose rulers didn't care a fig about what happened west of Iraq is the simple fact that throughout the Umayyad period, Iran and Iraq were governed by viceroys based in Kufa and/or Basra. No Umayyad caliph ever set foot in Iran. By contrast, Abbasid caliphs set foot in Egypt and the urban centers of Syria/Palestine on only the rarest and briefest of occasions.

This recital of differing Umayyad and Abbasid geographical orientations contains nothing new. But historians have generally held it to be unremarkable. It was just the way things were. Arabic-speaking Baghdad is only 450 miles from Arabic-speaking Damascus as the crow flaps its way across the desert, and the nomads on both sides of the intervening desert constitute the same mix of old tribes residing in the area under the Byzantines and Sasanids and new tribes that migrated from the Arabian peninsula with the Islamic conquests. Nevertheless, some historians are comfortable with the notion that the Umayyads felt especially close to the tribes of Syria while the Abbasids felt closer to the Arabs who had been sent to Iran in the conquest period and to the Iranians who converted to Islam. Hence the former looked west and the latter looked east. Others suggest that the sway of Byzantine tradition west of the Syrian desert was superseded by a love of Sasanid traditions manifested by the rulers to the east. But try as one might to explain the phenomenon away, the magnitude and consequences of the change in geographical orientation are fully equivalent to the Carolingian shift from a Mediterranean to a northern European orientation that served as the starting point for Pirenne's interpretive theory.

A deeper inquiry into the reorientation of the caliphate requires attention to three areas: the economy, the religious culture, and trade. Turning first to the economy, research I published in *Cotton, Climate, and Camels in Early Islamic Iran,* indicates a major transformation of the agricultural regime of the Iran's interior piedmont and plateau.[3] Before the Arab conquest, there is no concrete evidence of cotton being produced in this region, though it was known as a comparatively minor crop in the river valleys of Transoxiana. By 900, however, cotton growing and the sale of cotton cloth appear

---

3. Richard W. Bulliet, *Cotton, Climate, and Camels in Early Islamic Iran: A Moment in World History* (New York, 2009).

to have become the economic mainstay of forty percent of Iran's ulama. By comparison, just over twenty percent of the ulama of the Arab lands were involved in all aspects of textile production and trading. A few in Syria and Yemen dealt in cotton, but Egypt was at that time exclusively a linen producing land.

To simplify a complicated chain of argumentation, the Arab tribesmen who settled in Iran's interior piedmont zones, particularly those from Yemen where cotton had a long history, utilized local Iranian expertise in engineering and excavating underground canals (qanats) to bring water to uncultivated patches of desert. The technology was expensive, but the Arabs had accumulated substantial sums of money from war booty and the redirection of agricultural taxes from the Sasanid to the caliphal governors. Islamic law as it took form in the early Abbasid period granted these entrepreneurs freehold ownership of the "dead" land they brought into production in this fashion. The new agricultural initiative thus afforded the Arabs an unusual opportunity to become rural landowners in a vast country where the acreage irrigable by natural precipitation, seasonal runoff, or springs was already owned by indigenous Iranian petty gentry, who could not legally be displaced.

The staple crop of the indigenous farmers was winter wheat and barley. The long, hot summers were too dry for extensive cultivation. Qanats, however, provided a steady flow of water year round. This made summer cropping possible, and cotton became the most popular crop. Detailed information preserved in early Iranian sources indicate that the tax rate applied to cotton ca. 800 was double that for wheat and barley. By ca. 900 the differential was even greater as the tax on cotton was kept level while that on grain crops was greatly lowered. The heavy tax burden borne by cotton makes it clear that the profits earned by the cotton farmers were much greater than those earned by grain farmers. Value was then added to these profits by the spinning and weaving industries, which were centered in newly booming cities. However, migration to the booming cities changed the ratio of rural food producers to urban food consumers. This put pressure on the government to encourage food production, hence the lowering of the tax on grain.

Key to the Iranian cotton boom was the religious doctrine preserved in the *hadith* of the Prophet that pious Muslim men should never wear silk, the preferred fabric of the Sasanid elite. The Muslim ideal was to have Iranian converts to Islam dress like the Arab settlers in voluminous plain white or black gowns, robes, and headdresses. In Egypt and the Muslim west in general, linen served this purpose. In Iran and Iraq cotton was used. This form of dress received official caliphal endorsement in the form of government *tiraz* factories where long lengths of cotton or linen were ornamented with a two or three inch strip of silk embroidery and then fabricated into robes of honor given out by the caliphs as marks of prestige.

Because the Tigris and Euphrates rivers flooded wildly and unpredictably every spring when the snows of Anatolia melted, most farmers in Iraq could not easily practice summer cropping. Consequently, the Iranian cotton industry exported much of its production to Iraq. And of course the market for cotton textiles grew rapidly as conversion to Islam accelerated in both countries in the ninth century.[4]

Iran's urbanization differed from what was experienced in other regions. During the Sasanid period preceding the Arab conquest, small urban strong points, walled and garrisoned, had dotted the Iranian plateau. They afforded protection for traders, especially those plying the Silk Road that reached across Central Asia to China, but they seem to have manufactured little for export; and their size rarely exceeded 10,000 souls. However, between 800 and 1000, under the impetus of the cotton boom and the propensity of Iranian converts to Islam to migrate to the centers of Muslim activity, the largest Iranian cities swelled to the 100,000–200,000 range, making Iran one of the world's premier urbanized societies.

Muslim rule stimulated urban growth in other regions as well. But Iraq, Syria, Palestine, Egypt, Ifriqiya, and al-Andalus were much more urbanized than the Iranian plateau before the appearance of Islam. As a consequence, non-Muslim merchants and educated people came to play a more important role in urban-based cultural and commercial life in those Arab regions. Indeed, it seems likely that between Arab settlement in garrisons, the migration of Iranian converts from the countryside, and the dominant role of cotton grown and processed by Muslims in the trading economy, the cities of Iran came closer to being homogeneously Muslim than in any other region outside the Arabian peninsula.

This leads to the second area of inquiry, religious culture. Not only were all six of the Sunni canonical books of *hadith* compiled by Iranians, but information dealing with scholars traveling in search of *hadith* is overwhelmingly focused on Iran and Iraq. This could be simply an artifact of the survival of manuscripts, but two comprehensive compilations of scholarly biographies done in earlier centuries, one in the fourteenth (al-Dhahabi) and the other in the seventeenth (Ibn al-'Imad), show an identical preponderance of Iranian and Iraqi names.[5] This indicates that the sources that are available to

---

4. For the chronology of conversion in Iran, see Richard W. Bulliet, *Conversion to Islam in the Medieval Period: An Essay in Quantitative History* (New York, 1979), ch. 3–4.

5. This finding has been corroborated through analysis of other biographical collections in the doctoral thesis of Maxim Romanov.

us today do not differ significantly in content from those available in earlier centuries.

Looking specifically at the data taken from the Syrian Ibn al-ʿImad's collection, which covers a thousand years and is organized by death date, the share of eminent religious personalities apportionable to Egypt and Syria combined in his portrayal of the world of (Sunni) Muslim scholarship never exceeds 20 percent prior to the late Seljuq period. However, Iran alone has an average contribution of 40 percent for every quarter century period from 855/241 to 1097/491; and Iran and Iraq together account for at least 70 percent of the names from 758 to 1073.[6] Representation from al-Andalus and the western Maghrib during these centuries is negligible.

Regional representation among Muslim religious scholars

Dates	Total	IRAN	IRAQ	EG	SYR	EG+SY	Other
709/91	161	9%	46%	6%	12%	18%	27%
734/116	180	8%	61%	4%	13%	17%	14%
758/141	199	12%	62%	6%	12%	18%	8%
782/166	213	24%	54%	4%	10%	14%	8%
806/191	133	38%	39%	6%	13%	19%	4%
831/216	136	32%	48%	7%	4%	11%	9%
855/241	186	38%	39%	4%	10%	14%	8%
879/266	185	37%	39%	5%	12%	17%	7%
903/291	184	40%	36%	3%	10%	13%	11%
928/316	173	36%	42%	6%	8%	14%	8%
952/341	168	41%	32%	5%	10%	15%	12%
976/366	144	39%	31%	7%	12%	19%	11%
1000/391	123	51%	22%	4%	10%	14%	13%
1025/416	154	49%	29%	3%	6%	9%	13%
1049/441	127	39%	34%	4%	8%	12%	15%
1073/466	159	36%	33%	4%	11%	15%	16%
1097/491	151	32%	32%	5%	15%	20%	16%
1122/516	189	23%	37%	6%	20%	26%	14%
1146/541	193	23%	39%	7%	19%	26%	11%
1170/566	228	14%	29%	9%	38%	47%	10%
1194/591	192	6%	17%	11%	49%	60%	17%
1219/616	219	8%	12%	10%	60%	70%	10%

Multiplying examples of the disproportion between Islamic religious scholarship in the east and in the west would simply belabor the obvious. The conclusion is unavoidable that the turn to the east that began with Abu

6. The table was compiled from Abu al-Fath ʿAbd al-Hayy Ibn al-ʿImad, *Shadharat al-dhahab fi akhbar man dhahab*, 8 v., Cairo: Maktaba al-Qudsi, 1931–32. The dates shown on the table have been thrown back 60 years to approximate birthdates rather than death dates.

Muslim's pro-Abbasid uprising against Umayyad rule was not just political, but economic and cultural as well. The explosion of trade in Iran triggered by the cotton boom made travel by scholar merchants a normal practice. The cross-fertilization of religious and cultural outlooks that this brought about bore fruit in the burgeoning scholarly establishments of Iran's increasingly prosperous and predominantly Muslim cities.

Alas, climate deterioration evidenced by weather reports contained in chronicles and by tree-ring analysis carried out in Mongolia and Tibet devastated northern Iran's agricultural economy. It also contributed to the migration of Oghuz Turks from Central Asia into Iran. By the late Seljuq period, and even more strikingly in the succeeding Khwarazmshah period, Iran was suffering severe decline and an exodus of its scholarly elite to less affected areas like Syria, Anatolia, and India. As the above table clearly shows, the center of gravity of Islamic religious scholarship shifted dramatically toward Syria in the twelfth century.

To touch briefly on the third aspect of the east-west balance, trade, it need simply be noted that the Seljuq era also saw a good deal of the trade in the Persian Gulf shift to the Red Sea and to Egypt. This shift is symbolized by the disappearance of the Gulf port of Siraf as a major trading center after an earthquake in 977. The dynamism of the Iranian market for imported goods had fostered the growth of Siraf. But that dynamism waned shortly after the port's destruction, and the resulting contraction of the Iranian economy hindered the development of a substitute entrepot of similar scale. It should be noted that the migration of trade from the Gulf to the Red Sea antedated the growth of Mediterranean trade focused on cities in southern Europe that was a hallmark of the twelfth century.

In the history of Europe, the era of the crusades commands special attention. However, it is often noted that contemporary historical developments on the Muslim side were decidedly less scintillating. Yet this is precisely the time of the great shift back to the Mediterranean after four centuries of political, cultural, economic, and religious focus on Iran. Henceforward, the Levant would be the center of the Middle Eastern Islamic world with al-Andalus and the Maghrib rising to much greater prominence than before. All of these matters derive to a great extent from happenings that were centered in Iran.

By way of conclusion, I would like to return to the question posed at the outset. Was convivencia in al-Andalus in part a product of the comparatively non-controversial character of the Muslim religious community during the centuries when the most dynamic and conflict-producing developments in Islam were taking place far, far to the east? I believe that it was, and that

Islam's return to the Mediterranean that took place in the twelfth century introduced strains into the multi-communal synthesis of the west that had not been so strongly in evidence before that time. Whether this conjecture fits with the particulars of Andalusian history I must leave to others to decide. But regardless of their judgment, future explorations of the broad history of the Mediterranean lands under Islam should not be conducted without taking into account the history of Iran and the tidal currents that took Islam away from the Mediterranean in the eighth century and returned it again in the twelfth century.

Abu Muslim did not make Charlemagne possible any more than Muhammad did. But both names symbolize equivalent continent-spanning shifts in economic, political, and cultural centrality. Charlemagne moved the European center of political gravity northward; Abu Muslim moved the corresponding Muslim center of gravity eastward.

The History of the Muslim South:
The HajjJ and the Recentering of Islamic Civilization
(2008)

OST NARRATIVES OF ISLAMIC HISTORY note that the Prophet Muhammad was preparing a military expedition to the north at the time of his death in Medina in 632. Some of them take this as a harbinger of the subsequent northward direction of Muslim expansion under the Rashidun caliphs. As if in fulfillment of this predictive moment, stories of the Arab conquests include extensive descriptions of northerly expeditions to Syria, Iraq, Egypt, Iran, North Africa, Spain, and Sind while saying little about southern locales like Yemen and Oman or about Muslims reaching African, Indian, Southeast Asian, or Chinese ports by sea. Nevertheless, over the subsequent centuries, Islam had just as powerful an impact on lands to the south of the latitude of Medina as on lands to the north. The disproportion between the extensive accounts of events in the north and the meager coverage of events in the south is the topic of this essay. It will offer the conjecture that the Muslim south has been neglected by historians who equate Islamic history with the history of the Islamic state. Understanding and correcting this false equation can suggest useful insights regarding Islamic history as a whole.

Let us arbitrarily define the dividing line between the Muslim north and the Muslim south as 25 degrees north latitude, roughly the latitude of the first caliphal capital, Medina. (Medina actually lies at 24.5 degrees north latitude.) A look at today's political map reveals that by this definition the Muslim south, which includes sizable populations in Indonesia, Bangladesh, southern India, Malaysia, Nigeria, Guinea, Yemen, Oman, and Sudan, is home to at least as many souls as the Muslim north, somewhere around 700 million people.

Historiographically, the Muslim north tends to be treated as a comprehensive historical unit consisting of North Africa and Spain, the Middle East, Anatolia and the Balkans, Central Asia, Afghanistan, and northern India/Pakistan. Taking the caliphate(s) and such post-Mongol successor states as the Ottoman Empire, Safavid Iran, and Mughal India as a unifying narrative thread, historians see these northern areas as interacting significantly over time. Indeed, the only part of the Muslim north that is regularly exclud-

ed from this narrative scheme is China. The Muslim south, however, is not
treated as a politically interlinked region but rather as a series of discontin-
uous geographical areas: West Africa, East Africa, southern Arabia, Southern
India/Bangladesh, mainland Southeast Asia, and island Southeast Asia.

Yet the political history of the Islamic state, whether caliphate or sultanate, is not the same as the history of the Muslim faith community. To
be sure, the two histories corresponded closely in the earliest period, but
within three centuries significant erosion of caliphal unity had become
apparent. Moreover, the spread of Islam through conversion eventually created Muslim communities in lands that had never been subject to military
conquest by a Muslim power. Thus the history of the *umma*, the religiously
defined universal community of all persons who subscribe to the Islamic
faith, progressively separates from the history of the Islamic state.

Accounts of the institutional structure of Islam generally lay great
stress on the caliphate and emphasize that the regimes that succeeded the
weakening the caliphate in the Muslim north based their authority either
on a theoretical delegation of temporal caliphal authority in the form of a
sultanate (for example, Ghaznavids, Seljuqs), or on the idea of a counter-
caliphate (for example, Fatimids, Spanish Umayyads). Alternative bases of
political authority encountered in the Muslim south, such as the notions of
imamate propounded by Ibadi and Zaydi Shi'ite sects in southern Arabia, the
localized jihad states that propagated Islam through much of West Africa
from the time of the Almoravids onward, and such lightly Islamized traditional kingdoms as Acheh in Sumatra, are usually described as aberrant or
not mentioned at all.

If one substitutes the *umma* for the Islamic state as the focus of historical
inquiry, the propagation of the faith in areas that were not subject to conquest, such as Indonesia, Malaysia, East Africa, and China, presents several
problems. First, though specific narratives are often chronologically vague,
the spread of Islam in these areas seems largely to have taken place after
the year 1300. Indeed, it would appear that over half of all Muslims alive
today are descendants of people who converted after that date. Yet even
if one dismisses declarations about the post-Mongol "decline" of Islam as
tendentious and orientalizing, it is apparent that the most powerful Islamic
states of the post-1300 era, the Ottomans, Safavids, and Mughals, did not
play dominating political roles in the areas of the south where conversion
was most extensive. This highlights the disjuncture between the history of
the Islamic state and the history of the *umma*.

Secondly, the mechanism of Islam's spread in non-conquest areas, when
explored at all, has usually been looked at in localized terms or accounted

for by vague comments about "merchants and sufis." Thus the first half of the history of the growth of the *umma* reads as a byproduct of the expansion of the Islamic state, while the second half, though carrying equivalent demographic weight, reads as a series of local developments of mixed and uncertain causation.

Thirdly, while the idea of the *umma* retains its theological importance to the present day, in terms of real-world politics it seems to lose its geographical focus in the later centuries. The demise of Baghdad as the center of Islam in 1258, the year the Mongols destroyed the city and killed the last Abbasid caliph there, simply confirmed an erosion of the caliphate's loss of status as the effective center of the *umma* that had been underway for three centuries. From time to time in later centuries, one or another geographically peripheral Muslim land evinced a desire to consider the Ottoman Empire as a substitute for the caliphate. But these episodes were few and far between. Most outlying Muslim polities relied on their own resources and on the political traditions, both Muslim and non-Muslim, of their particular regions.

One way of reorienting historical thought for the second half of the history of the *umma* is to openly acknowledge that the Muslim south (and parts of the Muslim north, such as China), had little or no historical experience of the caliphate. Even such early-converting societies as Oman and Yemen remained largely aloof from the caliphate with their respective Ibadi and Zaidi imamates. For most other southern regions, conversion came about after the fall of the Abbasids. Even if the scholars in those regions knew that there had once been such an institution, an *umma*-wide caliphate was not part of either active memory or local Muslim tradition. Hence, it makes little sense to think of the caliphate, either theoretically or practically, as the core of the southern portion of the *umma*'s feeling of unity either before or after the thirteenth century.

What functionally replaces the caliphate as the center of the *umma* is the *hajj*, the annual pilgrimage to Mecca and Medina. As one of the five pillars of Islam, of course, the pilgrimage had always held a central place in Muslim religious consciousness. All Muslims were and are expected to participate in the ritual at least once during their lifetime if they are able. Moreover, the mention in historical chronicles – at least for the first several centuries – of the names of those appointed each year to supervise the pilgrimage (*amir al-hajj*) makes it clear that the ritual was fully under the jurisdiction of he caliphate.[1]

---

1. M. E. McMillan, *The Meaning of Mecca: The Politics of Pilgrimage in Early Islam* (St. London: Saqi Books, 2012), provides an excellent exposition of what the historical study of the pilgrimage in the early Islamic centuries can reveal about caliphal politics.

But between the twelfth and the fourteenth century, the ways the pilgrimage is referred to in historical sources undergo four important changes. First, the term Custodian of the Two Holy Places (*khadim al-haramain*) gradually becomes common in political parlance. Second, individual pilgrims, particularly in the Muslim south, adopt the practice of adding the epithet *hajji* or *al-hajj* to their personal names. Third, pilgrimage narratives appear as a significant literary form, along with, in some areas, pilgrimage certificates and Kaaba-centered maps. And fourth, multi-year sojourns in the holy cities for education and meditation replace the briefer pilgrimage stays of earlier times.

With respect to the first change, no caliph was ever specifically titled *khadim al-haramain*, even after the revival of the Abbasid house in Cairo after 1258, presumably because supervision of the pilgrimage had been assumed to be an inherent caliphal function ever since the caliphate began following the death of the Prophet. The title first occurs with Saladin (Salah al-Din al-Ayyubi) in a Syrian inscription of the late twelfth century, and it gained great importance under the Mamluk sultans who took control of Egypt and Syria after the fall in 1250 of the Ayyubid dynasty that Saladin founded. The Ottoman sultans picked up the title from the Mamluks when they conquered Egypt in 1516; and in 1982, three years after the brief but violent armed takeover of the grand mosque in Mecca by Juhayman al-Utaybi in 1979, King Fahd made it a part of the titulature of the ruler of Saudi Arabia.

Substantive changes accompanied the adoption of the new title. The last Ayyubid sultan took over what had hitherto been the caliphal duty of providing an embroidered cloth cover (*kiswa*) for the Kaaba, the cubical stone building in Mecca that serves as a focus of pilgrimage ritual. Furnishing the *kiswa* remained an Egyptian duty until the 1960s when King Abd al-Aziz b. Saud ordered that it henceforth be made in Saudi Arabia. Along the same lines, the rulers of Egypt – Ayyubids, followed by Mamluks, followed by Ottomans – formally took on the obligation of providing grain and other foodstuffs for the two holy cities. Under the Ottomans an additional function gained prominence, namely, the organization and provisioning of the annual pilgrimage caravan from Damascus. This latter practice led, in the late nineteenth century under Sultan Abd al-Hamid II, to the Ottoman government raising money by popular subscription to build a railroad from Damascus to the Haramain.

Taken together, these shifts of title and function relating to the pilgrimage constitute both a usurpation of a traditional caliphal role and a testimony to the enhanced importance of the *hajj*. A sultan could not claim the spiritual authority inherent in the title "caliph," but he could effectively replace the caliph as the facilitator and protector of a key pillar of Islam.

Moving from a grand title, *khadim al-haramain*, to a commonplace one, there is no way of determining when people first began to address returning pilgrims as *hajji* or *al-hajj*. However, a personal survey of more than ten thousand summary biographies of eminent Muslim religious figures who died before the year 1200 has not revealed a single instance of either of these titles being added to a name. Yet by the time of Ibn Battuta, whose famous travel account describes social life in many parts of the Muslim world in the early 1300s, the title had become fairly common. It subsequently became, and remains to this day, a highly esteemed marker of Muslim piety in a number of regions, particularly in the Muslim south.

The prominence of this title is undoubtedly connected with the final two indicators of the increasing importance of the pilgrimage, pilgrim narratives and extended sojourns in Mecca and Medina. Prior to the thirteenth century, scholarly biographies occasionally make mention of an individual frequenting (*mujawir*) the sacred places for a greater or lesser period of time, though not thereby acquiring the title *hajji*. There is even one instance of an eminent eleventh-century scholar, Abu'l Ma'ali 'Abd al-Malik b. 'Abd Allah al-Juwaini from Nishapur in Iran, who stayed for several years and served so prominently as a Sunni cleric at a time when Mecca was controlled by the Fatimid Shi'ite rulers of Cairo, that he earned the sobriquet Imam al-Haramain, or Imam of the two holy cities. But he is the exception that proves the rule.

In general, lengthy sojourns in the holy cities were uncommon, very possibly because of unreliable supplies of the food needed to support a sizable year round urban population. Unreliable provisioning might also explain why colleges of higher Islamic learning (*madrasa*) did not appear in Mecca or Medina until the late twelfth century. The great mosques in these cities had always functioned in part as educational institutions, but the advent of buildings dedicated to this purpose and generously financed through *waqf* endowments set the holy cities on track to become major centers for study, particularly for pilgrims, in later centuries. Almost from the beginning this educational enterprise resonated strongly with the Muslim south. Six of the first thirteen (out of twenty-three) Meccan *madrasa*s known for the period before the Ottoman takeover of Mecca and Medina in the sixteenth century were founded by Yemeni rulers or officials. Of the next ten, three were founded by rulers in India and three by local officials in the Haramain.[2]

Pilgrimage narratives testify to the importance of the *hajj* in the minds of Muslims. None are mentioned in the *Fihrist*, the famous list of books

---

2. Richard T. Mortel, "Madrasas in Mecca during the Medieval Period: A Descriptive Study Based on Literary Sources," *Bulletin of the School of Oriental and African Studies*, Vol. 60, No. 2 (1997): 236–252.

known to the late-tenth-century Baghdad bookseller Ibn al-Nadim. So it is likely that the one authored by Ibn Jubair about his pilgrimage from Spain in the 1180s, just after the establishment of the first *madrasa* in Mecca, was among the first. In later centuries, however, such accounts became common, particularly in outlying regions like Morocco and India.[3] Though some are contained within more extensive travel accounts, they all share the distinctive feature of having the Haramain as a fixed terminus. This became the lodestone of Muslim travel itineraries, imparting to them a unity that European travel narratives, which also became common in the post-Mongol era, generally lacked. Europeans typically wrote about traveling from a more or less common starting point, that is, someplace in Europe, to some far away exotic locale. Muslims, by contrast, wrote about traveling from many different spots in the far-flung Muslim world to a single, familiar place. While the novelty or "discovery" value of the European narratives has long been recognized, the degree to which the Muslim narratives continually reinforce the centrality of the *hajj* for the Muslim *umma* has not been accorded similar attention.

For believers living in the Muslim south, association with tens or hundreds of thousands of fellow pilgrims during the pilgrimage season, not just in carrying out the prescribed rituals but also in traveling together by ship or caravan, confirmed the reality of the notion of the *umma*. In some instances, it is possible to pinpoint the holy cities as exchange points for educational or doctrinal influences; for example, a Chinese pilgrim meets a Yemeni Sufi shaikh and brings a new understanding of Islam back home with him.[4] More generally, however, it must be assumed that all pilgrims were profoundly affected by their experiences and returned home to enriched spiritual lives.

Trade formed the inseparable counterpart of pilgrimage in the history of the Muslim south. Though in the early Islamic centuries there are reports and occasional archaeological traces of Muslim merchants here and there across the African Sahel and on the Indian Ocean littoral from East Africa to China, trade in the Muslim south expanded greatly after the eleventh century and kept on growing well into the era of European imperialism. Unlike the history of the *hajj*, this story, and the accompanying story of colonies of

---

3. See *Muslim Travelers: Pilgrimage, Migration, and the Religious Imagination* (Berkeley and Los Angeles: University of California Press, 1990), especially articles by Abderrahmane El Moudden and Barbara D. Metcalf.

4. For details about this example see Dru C. Gladney, *Muslim Chinese: Ethnic Nationalism in the People's Republic* (Cambridge, MA: Harvard University Press, 1991), 48–50. For similar accounts relating to Indonesia, see Azyumardi Azra, *The Origins of Islamic Reformism in Southeast Asia: Networks of Malay-Indonesian and Middle Eastern 'Ulama' in the Seventeenth and Eighteenth Centuries* (London: George Allen & Unwin, 2004).

Arabs from Yemen and Oman establishing themselves from Indonesia and Malaysia to Kenya and Zanzibar has received a good deal of attention. The same can be said of the role of Muslims in the growth of trade in sub-Saharan Africa, though the flow and social impact of African slaves mostly into other parts of the Muslim south requires more examination. Despite these studies, however, without the *hajj* as the centerpiece of the tale, trade history fails to convey the importance of human movement to the recentering of the *umma* after the demise of the caliphate.

In conclusion, even though the term "Muslim south" is purely arbitrary, it can serve to focus attention on a division between a history of Islam based on state institutions and one based on the human dimension of the concept of *umma*. Furthermore, by drawing attention to dynamic aspects of Islam in the post-Mongol era, it can help combat the stereotype of passivity so often ascribed to Islam in the later centuries. And finally, in the world of today where countries like Nigeria, Bangladesh, Malaysia, and Indonesia attract growing political attention, and population-poor but oil-rich Arabian lands have disproportional impact on the world economy, the study of the history of the Muslim south can appeal to students and scholars whose homelands participated only marginally in the history of the Muslim north.

The Arabian peninsula is a key world region because of its importance to the petroleum industry and its position in world finance. In Islamic terms, it is also a key region, though this perception is customarily limited to consideration of its historical role as the original home of the faith. If one adds to this the perspective of the history of the Muslim south, it becomes apparent that Arabia has for centuries been the geographical linchpin linking the Muslims of Africa with the Muslims of South and Southeast Asia. *Hajj*, trade, and human migration, including the vast numbers of southern Muslim guest workers currently employed in peninsular states, may provide an enlarged focus for understanding Arabia's longer-term historical role.

A further marker of how pilgrims perceive the contemporary centrality of Mecca may be seen in the construction there of the Mecca Royal Clock Tower Hotel, the world's second tallest building at the time of its construction. Just as the Ottomans replaced important buildings in the Haramain built by their Mamluk predecessors, so the Saudi kings have spatially supplanted the Ottoman sultans since assuming their title as Khadim al-Haramain.

The Siege of Vienna and the Ottoman Threat

(2014)

> Perhaps the interpretation of the Koran would
> now be taught in the schools of Oxford, and
> her pupils might demonstrate to a circumcised
> people the sanctity and truth of the revelation
> of Mahomet.
>
> Edward Gibbon on the possibility of
> Charles Martel losing the Battle of
> Tours to the Saracens in 732.[1]

IN 1521 THE ELECTORS OF THE HOLY ROMAN EMPIRE chose Charles V, the Hapsburg ruler of Spain, over Francis I of France as the imperial candidate most likely to press a successful war against the Ottomans. A month later, Ottoman forces took the Danubian fortress of Belgrade, and the following year the island of Rhodes, the eastern Mediterranean stronghold of the Knights of the Hospital of St. John. In 1526, at the Battle of Mohács, Sultan Süleyman the Magnificent's artillery annihilated the Hungarian heavy cavalry and killed their king, Louis II. He left no heir. Buda fell less than two weeks later, but Süleyman chose to withdraw leaving the Hungarian Diet to elect John Zapolya, the voivode of Transylvania, as tributary king. Two months later, an anti-Zapolya faction of Hungarian notables met at Pressburg (now Bratislava) further up the Danube to offer the throne to the Austrian Archduke Ferdinand, the brother of Charles V and of Marie of Hungary, Louis II's widow. The following year Ferdinand drove Zapolya out of Buda and took control of a narrow strip of Hungarian territory bordering Austria.

Ferdinand's aggressive actions, and pleas for aid from John Zapolya, provoked a return visit by Süleyman in 1529. The sultan and his army left Istanbul on May 10. On September 8, Buda again fell to the Ottomans, and Zapolya was reinstated as king. Despite the lateness of the season and the onset of autumn rains, Süleyman decided to take the war to Ferdinand. He reached Vienna with 120,000 troops, but without his heavy siege artillery, on September 27. Knowing that a relief force was on its way, Ferdinand pru-

---

1. *Decline and Fall of the Roman Empire*, New York: Bradley, nd, vol. V, 423.

dently retreated from his capital leaving a defensive garrison of 16,000 men. Ottoman siege operations against a courageous and vigorous defense lasted until October 16. Two months later, Süleyman was back in Istanbul unaware that the high point of Ottoman conquest in Europe had been reached.

Taking note of the bad weather and a German raid on Ottoman cannon and supplies being transported on the Danube, the authoritative Turkish historian Ismail Hakki Uzunçarsili concludes: "if it had been two months earlier [i.e. July] and the heavy cannon had arrived, there can be no doubt that Vienna would have fallen."[2] William H. McNeill's appraisal differs significantly. "Even at the beginning of Suleiman's reign (1520–66), the Turkish land frontiers had been pushed so far from Constantinople that the imperial field army lost a good part of its effectiveness. Sieges that had to be broken off after only a few weeks, like the famous beleaguerment of Vienna in 1529 ... were predestined to failure."[3] What Uzunçarsili seems to take into account, but McNeill ignores, is the fact that the second Ottoman siege of Vienna by an imperial field army from Istanbul commenced in July of 1683 rather than September, clearly demonstrating that distance alone was never a guaranteed protector of the city of Vienna.

Today the second siege of Vienna is generally considered a more important historical event than the first because it presaged the rollback of Ottoman power in the Balkans. But the theme of Ottoman decline did not always trump the theme of Ottoman expansion. Writing in 1915, for example, when the Ottoman Empire was a major power in World War I and the outcome of that war was still in the balance, D. G. Hogarth displayed the continuing mindset of Gibbon when he wrote:

> [T]he most brilliant and momentous of [Süleyman's] achievements ...
> was the conquest of Hungary. It would result in Buda and its kingdom
> remaining Ottoman territory for a century and a half ... and passing
> for all time out of the central European into the Balkan sphere; but
> also it would result in the Osmanli [i.e. Ottoman] power finding itself
> on a weak frontier face to face at last with a really strong Christian
> race, the Germanic, before which, since it could not advance, it would
> have ultimately to withdraw; and in the rousing of Europe to a sense
> of its common danger from Moslem activity. Süleyman's failure to
> take Vienna more than made good the panic which had followed on
> his victory at Mohacs. It was felt that the Moslem, now that he had

2. Uzunçarsili, Ismail Hakki, *Osmanli Tarihi*, Ankara: Türk Tarih Kurumu Basimevi, 1964, vol. II, p. 330

3. McNeill, William H., *Europe's Steppe Frontier 1500-1800*, Chicago: University of Chicago Press, 1964, p. 42

failed against the bulwark of central Europe, was to go no farther, and that the hour of revenge was near.[4]

Though the fortunes of war notoriously hinge on unforeseeable circumstances and chance occurrences, the 1529 siege of Vienna was a close enough call to justify the speculation that more clement weather might have tipped the balance in favor of an Ottoman victory. In pursuing this counterfactual speculation, however, it is important to make clear at the outset that I am *not* going to defend Gibbon's all-or-nothing scenario, his vision of a single critical battle in which Christian defeat eventuates in Muslims overrunning all of Europe and rooting out the Christian faith. Though the Ottoman armies were far better organized than the Muslim invaders of northern France that Gibbon wrote about, and their operations were part of a far superior political and strategic design, an Ottoman victory at Vienna in 1529 would no more have risked incorporating all of Europe in the domain of Islam than would a Saracen victory in that earlier semi-legendary conflict.

Instead I shall argue that the fall of Vienna to the Ottomans would have greatly intensified the political panic in Germany and provoked a clangorous demand among Lutherans and Catholics for Christian solidarity against the infidel, possibly forestalling the Thirty Years War. As importantly, the Hapsburgs would have lost their most valuable German territories and thus seen their influence greatly reduced. And finally, a prolonged Ottoman presence deep in German territory would eventually have forced western Europe to see the Muslim state more as a part of the European state system than as an "oriental" nemesis.

The argument as schematically proposed contains several second order counterfactuals. As the analysis proceeds, however, it should become apparent that the results of the first order counterfactual, an Ottoman victory at Vienna, need not be conceived of in a linear – A > B > C > D – fashion. Rather, I shall maintain that if a single, chance-driven, event is changed, the result is a node of uncertainty, a situation that could possibly resolve in several ways.

For example, Vienna might have been retaken in the following campaigning season. Or, the Ottomans might have sacked the city and withdrawn. Or, Ottoman forces might have used Vienna as a staging point for further penetration of the Danube valley. Or, German and Hungarian forces might have combined to cut off and destroy an Ottoman garrison left at Vienna after the sultan's return to Istanbul. One may also look farther afield. An Ottoman vic-

---

4. Hogarth, D. G., "Turkey," in Nevill Forbes et. al., *The Balkans: A History of Bulgaria, Serbia, Greece, Rumania, Turkey*, Oxford: Clarendon Press, 1915, pp. 338-9

tory against Archduke Ferdinand might have spurred his brother, Charles V of Spain, into some sort of retaliation in the Mediterranean. At a minimum, however, any of these immediate outcomes, or others that might be imagined, would have intensified the Christian panic and wrought changes in the texture of Catholic-Lutheran relations.

Of course, the counterfactual historian cannot just assert such an outcome. He must winnow the imaginable possibilities and choose the one (or several) that have the highest probability. Each choice becomes, in turn, a node of uncertainty that has to be addressed in the same fashion, with obviously increasing vagueness as one moves on to imagine third- or fourth-order counterfactuals.

To be at all useful, this sort of exercise must transcend personality. If the Ottomans had won the Battle of Lepanto in 1571, for example, Cervantes, who was present, might have been killed and *Don Quixote* might never have been written, leading to a markedly different history for the European novel. Probability and improbability at this scale are completely imponderable. It is only with larger groups and institutions that probability becomes assessable. But how large? Can one imagine with any plausibility, for example, a single event that would have altered the evolutionary trajectory from homo erectus to homo sapiens? The answer to this must be yes. A massive meteor strike could have terminated the entire primate line at any point in the past just as it could at any point in the future. Yet however stimulating this prospect might be to a writer of science fiction, historians engaged in counterfactual exercises must scale their speculations somewhere above the personal and below the cosmic. The nodes of uncertainty they conceive of must involve actors whose motivations are sufficiently known and general to be susceptible of plausible speculation, but sufficiently insulated from the vagaries of biographical detail to free the speculative endeavor from the impact of random chance.

Turning to the siege itself, Süleyman's war aims in eastern Europe seem clear from the series of campaigns he waged there. Time and again he led his armies up the Danube, reducing one fortress after another in an obvious effort to establish Ottoman dominance over the region. Though he considered the papacy to be his ultimate Christian foe, his objective in the Balkans was not so much a specific enemy as strategic control of territory. The strongholds he captured normally remained in Ottoman hands. With the exception of Ferdinand retaking Buda, which had been left under a weak tributary ruler, no Christian counterattack succeeded in regaining significant territory from the Ottomans until the latter half of the seventeenth century. The repeated test of battle, in other words, confirmed the superiority of Ottoman land forces on their western front throughout the sixteenth century. This fact must be taken into account in considering the most likely aftermath of a seizure of Vienna.

Since the history of Ottoman campaigns and strategy in the sixteenth century is not seriously in dispute, the immediate consequences of a victorious siege in 1529 seem easy to visualize. Given his mistake with Buda, Süleyman would not have withdrawn from Vienna without leaving behind a strong garrison. Given the lateness of the season, the Christian relieving force could have made little more than a token attempt to retake the city before retiring for the winter. The sultan would probably have spurned any suggestion of making Austria a tributary kingdom, as he had attempted to do with Hungary. Archduke Ferdinand, the rightful king, would still have been alive, making it all but impossible for an Ottoman-backed successor to effect a claim to legitimacy.

But would the Ottomans have waited a year and then continued on in subsequent campaigns with the intent of subduing the remainder of Europe? Historians' appraisals of the two failed sieges of Vienna bring this into question. Ottoman military campaigns began each year in Istanbul. Whether marching westward into Europe or eastward toward Persia, additional forces might be met en route; but the pace of the campaign was set by the main force coming from the capital. With no capacity to winter in the field, particularly in Europe, campaigns normally terminated with the onset of wet autumn weather. Thus a crucial factor for any Ottoman campaign in the sixteenth century was how long it took for the army to reach the frontier and confront the enemy. If the march to the frontier took several months, a delay to reduce a fortress or the early arrival of bad weather could stop a campaign before it had accomplished much. Several of Süleyman's post-1529 expeditions in Europe demonstrate this limitation. By this analysis, Vienna's location at the maximum Ottoman operational limit would have made a series of further expeditions into Bavaria or Bohemia unlikely.

A contrary scenario looks at how the Ottomans reacted to the failure and how Sultan Süleyman appraised his enemies. The 1530s saw major changes in Ottoman administrative practices. At Süleyman's accession in 1520, the empire had been divided into eight provinces governed by a *beylerbey*, the highest ranking provincial official. By 1544 there were eleven and at the end of his reign in 1566 twenty. Strategic considerations were central to this expansion, and it is not implausible to think that a successful siege of Vienna would have led the sultan to consider the upper Danube a spearhead penetrating the Christian heartland and to fortify and garrison it accordingly.

Süleyman, by this interpretation, was at heart personally absorbed in the dream of defeating the forces of the pope, valuing campaigns on his western frontier much more highly than those against Persia in the east.[5] Thus he might well have sought to use Vienna as a launching pad for further conquests in Germany, or across the Alps in northeast Italy.

Both of these projections are the product of hindsight, of course. At the time, fears of further Ottoman advance were beyond question. The fall of Belgrade in 1522 had touched off a cascade of anti-Turkish publications among both Catholic and Lutheran Germans. These have been intensively studied by John W. Bohnstedt, Kenneth Setton, and Stephen Fischer-Galati.[6] Bohnstedt's analysis, which for convenience we will be following here, makes it clear that regardless of its aftermath, an Ottoman seizure of Vienna in 1529 would have greatly intensified the existing fears. The first pamphlet, entitled *Türcken biechlin* (a South German dialectical version of *Türkenbüchlein* or "Turk-booklet") appeared a few months after Belgrade's fall. The anonymous author presents a discussion among a Turkish spy, his gypsy assistant, a worried Hungarian, and a Christian hermit. The spy boasts that the Sultan will soon make more conquests because the Christians are divided into feuding groups and the German soldiery wallow in drunkenness, gluttony, and indiscipline. To this the hermit confesses that it would be a good thing if the Christians enjoyed the unity and efficiency of the Turks, and opines that the Sultan's successes are God's punishment for sinful Christian deeds. He then calls on Europe's Christian kings to come to the defense of Hungary. This pamphlet was an instant bestseller. Seven editions appeared in 1522, and it was republished in 1527 and 1537.

In 1523 a Lutheran knight addressed a Turk-booklet to Pope Adrian VI, calling on him to abolish the papacy and devote the wealth of the Church to fighting the Turk. Next, just before the Battle of Mohács in 1526, came a tract urging the Germans to quit their factionalism and unite to face a potential Turkish attack. This went through numerous editions after the Hungarian defeat and was followed by an anonymous Catholic pamphlet, published in two editions, which asserts that the rise of Lutheranism has roused God's anger, of which the Sultan's triumph is a token.

5. I am grateful to Professor Cornell Fleischer for elucidation of this point of view.

6. John W. Bohnstedt, *The Infidel Scourge of God: The Turkish Menace as Seen by German Pamphleteers of the Reformation Era*, Transactions of the American Philosophical Society, N.S. LVIII/9 (1968); Stephen A. Fischer-Galati, *Ottoman Imperialism and German Protestantism*, 1521-1555, Cambridge, MA.: Harvard University Press, 1959; Kenneth Setton, *Western Hostility to Islam: and Prophesies of Turkish Doom*, Memoirs of the American Philosophical Society, v. 201. Philadelphia: American Philosophical Society, 1992

Luther himself chimed in with his treatise *On War against the Turks*, started in 1528 and published the following year. He, too, sees the Turkish menace as a divine punishment, but he advocates a strong defense led by the emperor rather than a Holy War sanctioned by the pope. Protestants generally deplored the temporal power exercised by the papacy in the form of crusades. But then came the siege of Vienna. Luther again put pen to paper, composing his *Military Sermon against the Turk*. Interpreting the Ottoman advance as an eschatological sign, he called again for vigorous defense and for prayer against the spread of Islam.

Lutheran tracts then multiply. A theology professor's description of the Turks as agents of Satan and a portent of the Last Judgement came out in 1529, after Luther's *Sermon*, and went through five editions. In 1531 there appeared Johannes Brenz's *Booklet on the Turk: How Preachers and Laymen Should Conduct Themselves if the Turk Were to Invade Germany*. It went though two editions that year, three in 1537, and one in 1542. The same author published his sermons against the Turks in 1532, and these too went through several editions down to 1538.

The Catholic pamphlets did not markedly differ. One published in 1529 called on all Germans to come to Austria's aid and portrays the struggle as a holy war. The following year Johan Haselberg took the same line, calling on Charles V to lead the Christian armies against the Ottomans. Two more Catholic Turk-booklets appeared in 1531 and another in 1532.

A new crop of pamphlets hit the bookstalls in 1541 and 1542 in response to further Christian setbacks. Luther's *Exhortation to Prayer against the Turk* (1541) demonstrates a deep worry about a possible invasion of Germany and advocates prayer for salvation from God's punishment and for the advent of the Last Judgement. Other Lutheran writers followed his lead while Catholic pamphleteers added their voices to the anti-Turkish chorus. These later tracts are outside the range of our consideration since we are proposing that a successful siege of Vienna in 1529 would have significantly altered the political landscape. They do, however, demonstrate the depth and persistence of Christian fears.

Here is a sample of Johannes Brenz's Lutheran rhetoric of 1537:

> Christians should also take comfort in the knowledge that the Turkish
> Empire is God's enemy, and that God will not allow it to annihilate
> the Christians. Although God has caused this empire to arise in these
> last times as the most severe of punishments, nonetheless He will not
> allow the Christians to succumb completely, and Mahomet will not
> rule alone in the whole world ... Therefore those who fight against
> the Turk should be confident ... that their fighting will not be in vain,

but will serve to check the Turk's advance, so that he will not become master of all the world.[7]

And this is a corresponding Catholic sentiment from a sermon of 1532:

> The attitude of the Christian fighters against the Turk should be as follows. They should fight not in order to gain great honor and glory, nor to acquire lands and possessions, nor out of anger and a desire for vengeance. Such motives are Turkish, not Christian, and one cannot vanquish Turks with Turks. Our warriors should fight in order to preserve and maintain, defend and protect, the name and honor of our Saviour Jesus Christ, and of His holy faith, which the Turk, its hereditary foe, is seeking to extirpate.[8]

More fevered presentiments of the end of days would not alone have pushed the course of history in a different direction. But the fall of Vienna would have had more material impacts as well, particularly on the circumstances of the house of Hapsburg. And a religious climate spiraling toward hysteria would certainly have amplified these political tremors.

Even if Vienna had not been the Hapsburg capital, it would have been of utmost strategic importance. The Marchfeld plain that surrounds it forms a corridor that connects the German lands to the west with the Hungarian and Slavic lands to the east. While the social, political, and religious outlook of Vienna was fully that of the Christian principalities of western Europe, the next important downstream city – called Pressburg by the Germans, Pozsony by the Hungarians, and Bratislava by the Slovaks—marked the frontier between western and eastern Europe. Beyond it lay the great central plain of Hungary, a land of steppes and marshes long used by Huns, Magyars, and Mongols as a route for invading western Europe. In 1500, its Magyar lords and oppressed Magyar, Slavic, and Rumanian peasantry constituted a sparse rural population. Its still undeveloped towns, whose trading potential was limited by the marshiness of the Danube and its tributaries, were populated mainly by Germans.

Vienna, therefore, was the key strongpoint separating Germany from the grasslands of Hungary; and no one was more aware of its strategic situation than the Hapsburgs. Since the Archduke Ferdinand whose assassination in Sarajevo in 1914 lit the fuse of World War I was a Hapsburg just like the Archduke Ferdinand who fled Vienna in 1529, we are accustomed to thinking of the Hapsburgs as timeless dynastic rulers. But their credentials were not so imposing five hundred years ago. From territorial origins in Alsace,

---

7. Bohnstedt, 44.
8. Bohnstedt, 48.

the Hapsburgs had gained possession, over several centuries, of Upper and Lower Austria along the Danube; the mountain lands of Styria, Carinthia, Carniola, and Tyrol to the south and west; and a southern corridor to Trieste and Istria on the Adriatic Sea. To the north lay the forested mountains of Bohemia, a much more potent kingdom in the fourteenth and fifteenth centuries. To the west was Bavaria, the powerful kingdom ruled by the Wittelsbach family.

The title of Archduke became formally established during the mid-fifteenth century when the Hapsburgs temporarily gained control of both Hungary and Bohemia, and several Hapsburgs were elected Emperor. Yet they were by no means the wealthiest or the most powerful of the German princes. After various ups and down, Hapsburg fortunes turned decidedly up at the end of the fifteenth century when Maximilian I succeeded his father Frederick III, who had been rather ineffective as Holy Roman Emperor. Maximilian retook Vienna from Hungary in 1493 and made a strategic marriage with the daughter of Charles the Bold of Burgundy.

This union not only brought the Hapsburgs new lands in the west but produced a son, Philip, who eventually married Joanna, the daughter of King Ferdinand and Queen Isabella of Spain. Their two sons, Charles and Ferdinand, were brought up in the Netherlands and in Spain, where teen-aged Charles inherited the throne in 1516 and took office as Holy Roman Emperor three years later. Charles then gave Ferdinand the family's Austrian territories in 1521, the same year Ferdinand married Anna, the sister of Louis II, the king of Hungary and Bohemia.

The point of this tedious narration is to demonstrate that as of 1529, Hapsburg power in Austria was neither overwhelming nor secure. Not only was Hapsburg wealth and might centered in distant Spain, but their eastern lands were closely hemmed in by neighbors: Bavaria, Hungary, and Bohemia. After the death of Louis II at the Battle of Mohács in 1526, of course, Ferdinand claimed the two latter crowns through his wife. As we have seen, however, Sultan Süleyman had his own candidate for the Hungarian throne and was able to reinstall John Zapolya in 1529.

Supposing counterfactually that the subsequent siege of Vienna had proven successful, what then would have been Ferdinand's situation? Politically, he would certainly have enjoyed the support and encouragement of other Christian monarchs, most notably his brother in Spain, who was marching to his aid. But where would he have stood geographically (and literally)? Without Vienna and the surrounding Marchfeld plain, the eastern Hapsburg territories would have been fatally split. The sparsely populated alpine provinces to the south and southwest could hardly have served as a base for a major counterattack, and the Bohemian lands to the north, only recently acquired, were riven by Catholic-Protestant animosity.

Ferdinand's immediate prospects after the loss of Vienna would have been bleak. Though young and vigorous, he would have lacked a strong territorial base for making a counterattack. Within this node of uncertainty, three possibilities stand out: first, a shrinkage of Hapsburg power in the east and fearful Christian acceptance of an Ottoman beachhead in western Europe; second, a mustering of Christian forces from Germany and beyond behind Ferdinand; or third, the launching of a potent Christian counterattack in the Mediterranean by Charles V, conceivably supported by his French rival Francis I.

The first course of events is not out of the question, given the historic feuding among the German princes. With an Ottoman salient splitting their lands, the eastern Hapsburgs might have faded away as a significant military power. Indeed, even with the successful repulsion of the Sultan's forces in 1529 and subsequent efforts to defend Christian territory, Hapsburg fortunes were not untroubled. As Kenneth Setton puts it: "In the years before and after 1600 the Hapsburgs were ... at the nadir of their history, and owing to Hapsburg ineffectiveness, the Turks were again a great menace."[9]

Moreover, the Ottomans were not unaware of the serious religious divisions among their Christian foes. An intelligence report sent to Süleyman in the summer of 1530 by an agent in Durrës (It. Durazzo) on the Albanian coast reported that Fra Martin Luther, the leader of a new sect opposed to the "false" rite of Catholicism, had raised an army of 30,000 men and routed Charles V's Spaniards in a battle at a place in Germany called San Borgo. The battle was a fantasy, of course; but the report shows a clear awareness of the virulence of the Protestant-Catholic divide. In addition, the intimation that Fra Martin Luther might command a major army against Charles V might well have suggested to Süleyman that the Protestants could be seduced into an alliance, just as in 1542 he briefly made common cause against Spain with Francis I.[10]

The actual course of events, however, makes an eclipse of Hapsburg power in the east seem less likely than the two suggested alternatives. Christian rulers did rally behind Ferdinand in a seemingly endless defensive war against the Ottomans, and the Mediterranean did become a cockpit of Mus-

9. Kenneth M. Setton, *Venice, Austria, and the Turks in the Seventeenth Century*, Philadelphia: The American Philosophical Society, 1991, 3.

10. Christine Isom-Verhaaren, "An Ottoman Report about Martin Luther and the Emperor: New Evidence of the Ottoman Interest in the Protestant Challenge to the Power of Charles V," *Turcica*, vol. 28 (1996): 299-317. I am grateful to Professor Cornell Fleischer for bringing this article to my attention.

lim-Christian strategic rivalry. The spate of anti-Ottoman pamphleteering that followed the Battle of Mohács would unquestionably have turned into a flood. Vienna lost! The Turk at the gateway to Germany! Christianity in peril! If the failure of the siege of 1529 provoked the Lutheran and Catholic outcry discussed earlier, a successful siege would surely have amplified it many-fold. And it is hard to imagine that Charles V and his French rival Francis I could have ignored the pressure to act.

A new crusade? The imagination need not be stretched so far. But there would surely have been a reappraisal of the Ottoman threat to western Europe, and plans would have been devised for countering it. One plan might plausibly have focused on Bohemia and Bavaria and aimed at a rollback along the Danube. Yet a strong Ottoman garrison in Vienna would surely have seemed like a tight cork sealing the Danubian bottleneck between the Alps and the Bohemian highlands. The Sultan's prosperous Mediterranean coastlands, his soft underbelly, would have seemed a more tempting target, and one easily reached from Spain without risk of French treachery. In fact, the Christian naval assaults launched in 1530 by the Italian admiral Andrea Doria, working for the Hapsburgs, were countered by equally skilled forces commanded by North African corsairs working for Süleyman. Nevertheless, the combination of a defensive strategy in central Europe and an offensive strategy in the Mediterranean seems perfectly plausible, since that is more or less what actually transpired.

Such is the dilemma of the counterfactual historian. Knowledge of what really happened tends to make the outcome that deviates least from the record of subsequent historical events seem the most plausible. Second-order counterfactuals that radically depart from that record tend to sound hyperbolic, if not absurd. Yet a node of uncertainty truly is uncertain. Unlike a gyroscope that resists perturbation because of the physical properties of a spinning object, single events can trigger dramatic historical changes that in hindsight would have been declared impossible to predict.

Thus despite the attractiveness of seeing an Ottoman seizure of Vienna as simply a relocation of the Christian-Muslim frontier a bit farther up the Danube, and a consequent intensification of the Christian will to resist both in central Europe and the Mediterranean, the possibility of a major shift in the European balance of power seems even more likely.

Assuming that Süleyman would have placed a powerful, indeed an invincible, garrison in Vienna; and further assuming that he would have had the vision to reorganize his territories and his forces to concentrate more intensively on confronting the papacy, a significant Muslim presence in Germany would most likely have become a fact of European political life.

What would the longer term consequences have been? Without trying to detail a series of third-order counterfactuals, it is fair to conjecture the following: The rollback of the Ottoman empire that got underway late in the seventeenth century under Hapsburg leadership would have been delayed, or never would have occurred. A strategic resettlement of Muslims in Vienna, followed more slowly by religious conversion of some of the natives, would have brought into being a significant German-speaking Muslim population. A cosmopolitan Vienna would have bridged the cultural divide between eastern and western Europe and served as a conduit for the transmission of western European ideas and practices into Ottoman lands, a phenomenon well attested in Istanbul itself at the beginning of the eighteenth century.

More intriguing than any of the foregoing is the likelihood of the Ottomans becoming an active player in the drama of Reformation. Without going so far as to suggest that the sultans would have championed the Protestants against the Catholics, there is nothing implausible in the notion that either Catholic or Protestant princes might have sought tactical advantage by soliciting Ottoman support. After all, the history of the crusades is replete with tactical alliances between Christians and Saracens.

In the long run, this last possibility adumbrates a European future in which the Ottoman Empire becomes accepted as a "normal" part of the continental balance of power and never experiences the conceptual relegation to a position of "oriental" inferiority that became increasingly evident in the eighteenth century. And as a corollary of such an acceptance, this alternative future might have seen individual Muslims, speaking German and perhaps other western European languages, visiting or living as normal people on the Christian side of the frontier. However farfetched such fraternization across a European Muslim-Christian divide might seem, today's nearly universal harmony between Protestants and Catholics would have seemed equally unthinkable to Germans fated to live out their lives during the Thirty Years War of the seventeenth century.

With the establishment in the 1990s of the Centre for Islamic Studies at Oxford, Gibbon's horrified imagining of the interpretation of the Koran being taught in the schools of Oxford, and her students imbibing "the sanctity and truth of the revelation of Mahomet" ironically and peaceably came to pass. It didn't require the conversion of Europe by the Saracen sword to make it happen; the aftermath of imperialism and the advent of oil money did the trick. By the same token, it should not be assumed that the eighteenth and nineteenth century "orientalizing" of the Muslim world, most notably in the guise of the Ottoman Empire, was unavoidably determined by fundamental matters of faith. If the summer of 1529 had been a bit drier and the Ottoman siege cannons had kept on schedule, the trials Christians and Muslims in Europe are now experiencing in learning how to live together might have been weathered two or three hundred years ago.

9/11: Landmark or Watershed

(2011)

WAS 9/11 A LANDMARK EVENT OR A WATERSHED EVENT? I started posing this question to friends and students soon after the attacks on the World Trade Center and the Pentagon and urged them to keep it in mind as they watched the fallout from that event over the passing years.

My definition of a landmark event is something that stands out on any historical chronology in the way a church steeple stands out on a physical horizon, orienting riders in a steeplechase. It's highly visible, but in the broad sweep of history perhaps not truly consequential. Pearl Harbor is an example. Given the ongoing war in Europe and America's commitment to supporting Hitler's enemies, it was highly likely, and was popularly perceived at the time, that the United States would have entered World War II at some point even without the Japanese attack on its Pacific fleet. Pearl Harbor sparked a declaration of war, but the powder keg was primed and ready to blow.

My definition of a watershed event is something that fundamentally changes the direction of things, just as a physical watershed marks the point where river waters divide, draining toward the Mississippi River, say, on one side and toward the Atlantic Ocean on the other. The Bolshevik October Revolution fits this definition. Before it occurred, Russia's revolution was following a pattern of other anti-monarchical movements that had broken out here and there in Europe ever since the French Revolution. It was a landmark event. After the October Revolution, however, every government action flowed toward the establishment of an unprecedented socialist state and empire, thus making it a watershed event.

Up until 2008, most people I posed my question to preferred watershed to landmark. Then came the collapse of the housing bubble and the resulting economic crisis. Now when I ask people which is historically more important, 9/11 or the 2008 economic crisis, I find there is no consensus. Could both be watersheds? If the flow of history changed in 2001, as the term watershed implies, is it comprehensible to think of it changing direction again just seven years later? The question calls to mind a dilemma of the first half of the twentieth century. Some sensitive artistic souls maintained that the horrors of World War I had made art philosophically impossible. Thirty years later some of the same souls maintained that the horrors of the Holocaust made art philosophically impossible ... again. How often can everything change completely?

Only seven years separate 9/11 and the collapse of the housing bubble in 2008. Today's college freshmen weren't even born when the twin towers fell, but many of them are living today in homes with mortgages that are underwater and are aware of the anguish of parents who lost jobs in the Great Recession. When the twentieth anniversary of 9/11 comes, college freshmen will know about the terrorist attacks only through history books and old videos, but they may still be living in desperate economic times.

One way to answer my question would be to say that the passage of time turns all watersheds into mere landmarks, but that will not do. The Emancipation Declaration has retained its watershed quality. So has the dropping of atomic bombs on Hiroshima and Nagasaki. So has the assassination of Archduke Ferdinand in 1914.

My own answer to the question is that 9/11 was indeed a watershed event, and the economic collapse of 2008 in large part a consequence of the new direction in which history has flowed in its aftermath.

Before 9/11 the United States was in an optimistic frame of mind. Bill Clinton had been reelected and was enjoying the luxury of a major budgetary surplus. The Dayton Accords had started to defuse the turmoil of post-Soviet Yugoslavia. Iran had a liberal president and cautious feelers that might eventually lead to reconciliation with the United States had been exchanged. The Dow Jones Industrial Average was hitting historic highs, and home sales were booming as Americans optimistically took on more and more debt. In popular culture, good guys, like Kurt Russell in the movie *Executive Decision* (1996) and Arnold Schwarzenegger in *True Lies* (1994), still acted just in time to prevent the nuclear incineration of an American city.

Then came 9/11, and the water started to flow in a different direction. Any president would have responded to the attacks with military action. And given the fact that the Bush and the Gore presidential campaigns both had deep concerns about Saddam Hussein still being in power in Iraq a decade after Desert Storm, there is no way to be sure that a Gore administration would not have targeted Iraq, either sooner or later. It also seems likely that any president, observing the country's day-after economic nosedive, would have urged Americans to carry on as if they had not received a powerful blow to the solar plexus. The cliché of the time was: "If we don't do X, the terrorists win." If you were planning to buy a house, go ahead. Don't let a bearded freak in a cave in Afghanistan bring us to our knees.

So the unique circumstances of 9/11, a devastating attack on the world's greatest superpower by a secretive gang of fanatics, diverted the flow of American, and thus world, history. The United States declared war on an enemy it could not locate, and fought the war on the soil of an enemy that had not been involved in the attack. Even though the war was radically asymmetrical, the cost of the war was comparable to other major conflicts in American history. Yet if the president, any president, had asked his fellow Americans to hunker down, put their shoulder to the wheel, donate their children's lunch money to the national war chest, and show in their day-to-day living just how badly they felt they had been hurt by the towers' fall, the terrorists would have won, at least by the logic of the day. It was terribly important that the war should be fought at the level of skill and armament that the United States alone, of all the world's nations, was capable of; but it was equally important that the war effort should not be allowed to erode, or to erode further, the American sense of well-being.

Whatever one believes about the roots of America's current obsession with government spending and the national debt, there can be no doubt that extraordinary military expenditures with no counterbalancing revenue streams contributed mightily to the problem. Nor can it be assumed that Albert C. Gore, if he had been elected president, would have either confined the war expenditures or persuaded Congress to raise the tax revenues required to see the effort through to a successful conclusion. If the United States had not gone after the terrorists wherever they were (or weren't, as was so often the case), the terrorists would have won. If the administration had imposed a war tax and instilled a sense of wartime self-denial in the minds of the public, the terrorists would have won.

Did the desire to keep the good times rolling contribute to the country's financial crescendo and collapse? I believe it did. If public and private expenditures had been held in check, after all, the terrorists would have won. For surely the selection of the World Trade Center proved that the ultimate objective of al-Qaeda was to bring the United States to its knees financially. Spending money and taking on debt proved that Osama bin Laden could not succeed in his fiendish plan.

While all this was going on in the world of politics and finance, the national mood soured. To be sure, the housing crisis and the tanking of almost everyone's retirement dreams played a role, but the change in mood began before 2008. In popular culture, it now became commonplace to begin a movie or television show with a murderously successful terrorist (or supposed terrorist) attack. In the television series *Jericho* (2006), twenty-three American cities suffer nuclear annihilation in the first ten minutes, leaving a small town in Kansas to fend for itself. The series *Battlestar Galactica* (2004–2009) not only begins after the near annihilation of the human race, but integrates terrorist suicide bombing, carried out by the good guys, into its narrative. In *Terminator 3: The Rise of the Machines* (2003) no amount of heroism can stave off the nuclear holocaust that was held in abeyance in the first two *Terminator* movies. The list is nearly endless.

Less entertainingly, despite President Bush urging Americans not to take their anger out on innocent Muslims, the tide of Islamophobia has grown stronger every year since 9/11. And with it have come powerful reaffirmations of Christian righteousness, and repudiations of anything Islamic, on the part of major political contenders. Some historians were aware of the potency of Islamic political reassertion at the end of the twentieth century, but no one predicted that the twenty-first century would be born in such an atmosphere of born-again Christianity and interfaith (as opposed to Samuel Huntington's intercivilizational) nastiness.

Obviously, American reactions to 9/11 did not cause the 2008 financial crisis. But it is hard to imagine that absent 9/11 and the ensuing "war or terror," which has metastasized into today's Islamophobic fight against "radical Islamic terrorism," a continuation of the Clinton boom era would have turned into an equivalent trainwreck. And it is hard to imagine that the negativity that is so evident in almost all areas of American life today would have been so pronounced if 2008 had produced a run-of-the-mill recession unsalted by the sour and gloomy attitudes that took root in the devastation of the World Trade Center.

The financial crisis certainly brought more ruin upon the country than the 9/11 attacks. But 9/11 jarred a happy land out of its complacency, and history has flowed in a different direction ever since.

So the terrorists won.

A Wild Tomb Chase
(2017)

IN 1966 I RAN ACROSS A PECULIAR TOMBSTONE in the ruins of the medieval Iranian city of Nishapur. The conjectures this "discovery" prompted touched upon my pride as a historical detective, my claim to having insights on contemporary Iranian affairs, and my far from stellar career as a novelist.

Once an "Aha!" moment occurs there is no telling where it can lead.

Me In Iran

In April, 1977, at the end of my first year teaching at Columbia University, the Director of the university's Middle East Institute, Professor J. C. Hurewitz, offered to have the Institute pay for me to participate in a "scholar-diplomat seminar" in Washington, D.C. Hurewitz had a long and fruitful relationship with the US Department of State, and I'm sure he felt that my teaching about the modern Middle East would benefit from observing its operations firsthand.

Iran was my primary interest. During two years of teaching at the University of California at Berkeley before coming to Columbia, I had become increasingly convinced that what we have come to call Islamic politics was a growing force that would soon overtake all of our scholarly concerns about nationalism, socialism, and modernization. This conviction arose partly from looking at the long-term trajectory of Islamic history and partly from conversations with various colleagues, most notably Hamid Algar and Hichem Djaït. With that in mind, I asked Frank Huddle, a former student who was the Iran desk officer in the State Department's Intelligence and Research division (INR), whether he had any materials relating to Ayatollah Khomeini. He said he thought there were a couple of pamphlets, but he told me that the bank of filing cabinets devoted to Tudeh, the Iranian communist party, was the proper archive for me to explore. I disagreed.

The following fall I received an invitation to attend a large conference in Hamadan devoted to the history of government administration in Iran. I flew to Tehran with my friend from Harvard, Roy Mottahedeh, both of us among the most junior conference invitees, and then traveled to Hamadan by bus. The conference was not memorable intellectually, but it gave me a chance to listen to senior scholars like Bertold Spuler, Hans Robert Roemer, and Masashi Haneda whom I would never again meet. Otherwise the trip to Iran, my first since 1971, provided an opportunity to talk to various Iranians and to observe the state of Iranian society, both in Tehran, where the Tehran University campus was being patrolled by the military, and in the provincial city of Hamadan.

When I got home and read the news about disturbances in Iran, the thought slowly grew in my mind that a religious revolution against the shah was more than an idle speculation.

The Tombstone

At the conference I made the acquaintance of Dr. Hossein Modarressi, a vastly learned member of the Shi'ite clergy who has since become a professor at Princeton University. Back in New York, it occurred to me that Dr. Modarressi might solve a problem that had been vexing me for a long time. It concerned a gravestone inscription that I had happened upon during my first visit to the ruins of medieval Nishapur in 1966. One day I spotted a meter-tall white memorial column (called an *imamzadeh*) sticking up at the distant edge of a farmer's field next to the railroad track running from Tehran to Mashhad. When I made my way over to it – no path led in that direction – I saw no other gravestones and no evidence that anyone had recently visited the spot. Moreover, though the small stone set into a niche in the *imamzadeh* was obviously quite new, with fresh, sharp edges to its clumsily carved letters, it didn't look or read like the many modern gravestones I had looked at during my stay in Nishapur.

The portion of the inscription I could read was garbled and mixed Arabic words with Persian words, using both *ibn* and *farzand* (for "son of"), for example. Moreover, the funerary formula closely echoed medieval gravestones – it began: *hadha mashhad al-marhum al-Husain al-Makfuf* [the Blind] *ibn Zaid...*, meaning "This is the shrine of the late Husain the Blind, the son of Zaid...." – and it bore the remarkably early death date of 124 AH, the equivalent of 741–42 CE. The date was written out in Persian (*yak sad o bist o chahar*) instead of being given in numerals as has been the common Iranian practice for at least the last five centuries. Genuine Muslim tombstones of that purported date would have had the date written out in Arabic (*mi'a wa 'ishrin arba'a*). I copied the inscription down as best I could.

The scrap of paper with my copy of the inscription reemerged during my move from Berkeley to New York in 1976, and I discovered that I could now read it in full. The person memorialized (though supplied in the inscription with the wrong mother) was unquestionably the son of the Shi'ite

Imam Zaid b. ʻAli Zain al-ʻAbidin b. al-Husain b. Ali b. Abi Talib, who was killed while leading an uprising in Syria in 740. Al-Husain b. Zaid, who reportedly went blind late in life, had a brother named Yahya who was killed a year or so after his father under similar rebellious circumstances. Al-Husain is also reported by some sources to have had a son named Muhammad, called al-Mahruq ("the Burnt") because of the alleged burning of his remains. Muhammad Mahruq had raised an unsuccessful revolt in Iraq in 815 and then been transported (living or dead?) to Khurasan, the province of which Nishapur was then the paramount city.[1]

Here is the account of the death of al-Husain's brother Yahya contained in Clifford Edmund Bosworth's *The Ornament of Histories*, a translation of Abu Saʻid Abd al-Hayy Gardizi's eleventh-century Persian language chronicle *Zayn al-Akhbar*.

> When [the Umayyad caliph] Hisham died, Walid b. Yazid succeeded to power. He sent an investiture charter for [the governorship of] Khurasan to Nasr b. Sayyar and commanded him to capture Yahya b. Zayd. When Yahya came to a rural district of the administrative region of Nishapur, he threw off allegiance to Walid and summoned people to his own cause. He went back with 120 men and encamped at a village by the gate of Nishapur. ʻAmr b. Zurara al-Qasri, the amir of Nishapur, sent an envoy to Yahya with a message, "Get out of this district!" Yahya replied, "[I'll stay here] until I have rested and the beasts have rested!"
>
> When he drew near to ʻAmr, the latter immediately mounted and rode forth. They clashed in battle, ʻAmr was defeated and in the course of his flight was killed. Yahya b. Zayd headed for Balkh [the center of Umayyad military power in Khurasan]. When Nasr got news of these events, he sent his police commander (sahib-shurat) Salm b. Ahwaz in pursuit of Yahya. Yahya went to Badghis and from there to Marw al-Rud, Talaqan and Faryab. Salm pursued him continuously until he came upon him at Arghuy in Guzganan. A battle was fought and Yahya b. Zayd was killed. His head was cut off, mounted on a pole and borne to Merv.[2]

I was quite excited by identifying al-Husain the Blind's (fake?) tombstone because it fit so well with the story of his brother Yahya continuing

1. Genealogies disagree. The citation of al-Husain as Muhammad al-Mahruq's father, instead of the usual genealogy, which gives his father's name as Muhammad, is sourced to Sayyid Ahmad Yazdi Ardekani of Nusaybin, a specialist on Shiʻite genealogy, on the website: abarshahr.blogfa.com/post-99.aspx (retrieved July 2017).

2. Abu Saʻid ʻAbd al-Hayy Gardizi, *The Ornament of Histories: A History of the Eastern Islamic Lands AD 650–1041,* tr. and ed., C. Edmund Bosworth, London: I. B. Tauris, 2011, 27.

their father's revolt in Khurasan. My conjecture was that Yahya took his blind brother – was he blind by that time? – with him to Nishapur when he fled the battlefield after this father's defeat in Syria.

By the time I had determined al-Husain the Blind's full identity, I had also evolved a conjecture as to why the tombstone purporting to date from the mid-eighth century was so new and so crudely executed. According to my topographical reconstruction of the ruins of Nishapur, the gravestone was located at a point where the railroad, which was built earlier in the 1960s, could have passed through an important medieval cemetery. Since the track was laid in a cut about ten feet deep, I surmised that an ornate inscription marking the grave of Yahya's brother al-Husain had accidentally been destroyed in the building process. Faced with the dilemma of whether to report the destruction of an important antiquity and risk a delay in their building schedule, or to ignore it and risk a charge of sacrilege if someone else reported it, the builders decided to summon an unskilled stone-carver and someone who could decipher a medieval Arabic inscription. They copied the gist of what they could read on the destroyed stone, and placed the copy in an isolated *imamzadeh* beside the track. Then they moved on and told no one in Nishapur what they had done. That is why the Arabic phraseology was that of a medieval stone. As for the date, it would have been written out in Arabic on the original stone, so the carver was told to write it out, which he did in Persian. Inquiries I made in Nishapur turned up no one who had ever heard of the *imamzadeh*. This confirmed in my mind the notion that the stone had been carved in secret and left behind as the railway builders moved on.

What To Do

Not wanting to make a scholarly publication based on such a conjecture, which depended so heavily on what might have happened in the building of the railroad, I nevertheless felt that the stone was potentially of importance for Iranian Shi'ites since it involved an early direct descendant of the Prophet Muhammad's cousin Ali b. Abi Talib. After all, the major cities of Mashhad and Qom in Iran and Mazar al-Sharif in Afghanistan are all centered around the tombs of early members of the family, and one of Cairo's most celebrated mosques commemorates Yahya b. Zayd's sister Zainab.

So I communicated my conjecture to Dr. Modarressi in a letter, and he sent me two lengthy responses. In the first, he informed me that the burial place of al-Husain the Blind is uncertain, being variously reported in Shi'ite religious works, but that Nishapur is not mentioned as a possibility. His date of death is also uncertain, though the possibilities mentioned in the Shi'ite sources cluster right around 124 A.H./741–2 CE. In his second letter, Dr. Modarressi stated that on reflection, he had concluded that I had most likely run into a pious fraud perpetrated by someone in Nishapur who believed he had "discovered" the forgotten tomb of a saintly descendant of Ali, possibly via a dream in which al-Husain the Blind or one of his relatives had appeared. In sum, he felt that the early Shi'ite religious texts would have mentioned al-Husain the Blind's Nishapur resting place if it had ever existed. Hence the gravestone was of no importance.

Having done my duty in reporting the tombstone to an eminent Shi'ite cleric, I now felt free use the information I had uncovered as I wished. Nevertheless, while I recognized that frauds of this type are not unknown in Islamic history, I could never square Dr. Modarressi's theory with the *imamzadeh*'s isolated location by the railroad track, the crude and garbled character of its carving, its medieval phraseology and written-out death date, and the fact that the people I talked to in Nishapur knew nothing about it. Why would someone have perpetrated a fraud of this kind just a few years previously when the train track was being laid and then have done nothing to publicize it?

Throughout the spring of 1978 I thought about the tombstone as I read newspaper accounts of what was happening in Iran. Slowly my notion that Iran was ripe for a religious revolution merged with the thought that a millenarian movement based on the discovery of a religiously significant medieval tomb could, in a fictional universe, be a catalyst for such a revolution. By early June, the plot of *The Tomb of the Twelfth Imam* was well in mind, and I finished writing the novel in August, shortly before the Zhaleh Square massacre on September 8 kicked the simmering revolution into a higher gear.

I telephoned Joan Kahn, the Harper & Row editor who in 1973 had selected my first novel, *Kicked to Death by a Camel*, for publication, and she told me to send the manuscript to her by messenger. Then I heard nothing for several weeks, which wasn't too surprising since she had (rightly, I think) rejected the two manuscripts I had sent her in the intervening years. So I telephoned her again, and she told me that what I had written was so close to what seemed to be actually going on in Iran that they were afraid their readers would be confused. She remarked that there had recently been an earthquake in Iran but there was none in my manuscript. I replied that there was no earthquake because what I had written was fiction, but I would be happy to add to the manuscript a Prologue set in the eighth century in order to make it clear that my work was pure fiction. She accepted that plan.

Harper & Row was clearly uncomfortable with my book. Their entry into the competition for the first insightful book about the Iranian Revolution was William H. Forbis, *Fall of the Peacock Throne*, which the author had obviously begun as a tribute to the shah's wonderful regime and then finished by tacking on a chapter or two to account for what the rest of the book had indicated was an inexplicable rejection of a model sovereign. My novel was the only book at the time to talk about religious politics in Iran and the only one to visualize a religiously based revolution. By the time Harper & Row finally saw it into print, however, with no special publicity, the embassy hostage crisis had begun and I had lost my potential audience. Almost a year and a half had elapsed since I had finished the writing. A few months after *The Tomb of the Twelfth Imam* appeared, I had a stiff exchange of letters with a senior editor at Harper & Row and severed my relations with the company.

Despite a few fairly positive reviews, it was painful for me to read in the Los Angeles Times:

> Oooops. Talk about the wrong time and the wrong place .... One can picture [the author], visions of a best seller, not to mention movie rights, dancing in his eyes.... However, for reasons all too painfully clear, the current crisis hasn't prompted a great movement to plumb the Moslem mind. How often do you hear, for example, someone saying: "You know, I'd really like to take an Iranian to lunch to understand how they really think"? ... It's not that bad, but we're not watching "War and Peace" go down the tubes.[3]

I confess that *The Tomb of the Twelfth Imam* is far from being a literary masterpiece, but I believe it captured an important historical moment and situation that Americans otherwise missed ... and are still missing. At the end of the Afterword I wrote: "Questions aside, whether fraudulent or genuine, this stone or another, the appearance of a catalyst for transforming religious expectation of the Twelfth Imam's reappearance into political action is always a possibility in Iranian Islam. It has happened in the past; it can happen again. No government is immune to destruction by this means."

I have been ridiculed for suggesting that my novel "foresaw" the Iranian Revolution. It didn't. Yet there weren't any other books written six months before the shah fled into exile that described a clergy-led movement to overthrow him.

Back to Nishapur

In the Spring of 2016 I spent two days in Nishapur for the first time since I had discovered al-Husain the Blind's putative tombstone fifty years before.

---

3. "The Wrong Time, Wrong Place," *Los Angeles Times* (Dec. 10, 1979).

I suspected that no one in Nishapur, save a scholar or two, had ever read my various writings about their city. But then the governor and some professors from the University of Nishapur met the plane. A parade in my honor progressed between children lined up to present flowers and welcomes to the elegant monument to Omar Khayyam, whom everyone believes to have been buried on the adjoining grounds of the beautiful seventeenth-century shrine to Muhammad Mahruq. Officials gave speeches; I gave a speech.

Eventually a crowd led/accompanied me back to the ruins, which, it turned out, had been preserved from Nishapur's otherwise exuberant urban development because of a map I had published showing the great extent of the medieval city. Discovering that my writings had given the citizens of Nishapur a luminous history for which they were bounteously grateful moved me almost to tears.

But what about the mysterious tombstone? I had assumed that the doubt that Dr. Modarressi had cast on my conjecture about its origin and importance almost forty years earlier had caused it to be removed. When I asked one of the caretakers, however, he told me that it is still in place. But visiting it is prohibited because: "It has not been authenticated."

Hallelujah! My conjecture lives. Someone, somewhere in the Shi'ite clerical establishment seems to think that I may possibly have been right.

Location, Location, Location

My return visit to Nishapur reawakened the unresolved question of why Omar Khayyam's grave, and his adjoining monument, seem to be located nowhere near where he was actually buried. The author Nizami Aruzi, who knew Omar personally, provides the only direct testimony regarding his burial. The eminent Iranologist A. V. W. Jackson translated the passage as follows:

> When I came to Nishapur in the year 530 AH [1135 CE] – it being four years since that great soul had drawn on the veil of dust and the inferior world had become orphaned of him – I went on Friday eve to visit his tomb, because he had upon me the claim of a master. I took with me some one who could point out his grave and he took me out to the Hirah Cemetery. I turned to the left and saw his grave located at the end of the garden-wall.[4]

There is no reason at all to doubt this report. Nizami Aruzi knew Omar Khayyam and admired him as a scientist and astronomer. He availed himself

4. A. V. W. Jackson, *From Constantinople to the Home of Omar Khayyam*, London: Macmillan, 1911, pp. 241-42.

of a local guide to find the tomb. Hira cemetery was possibly the best-known burial ground in the city. And in 1135 Nishapur had not suffered the terrible cataclysms that would leave the city in ruins and cause its surviving inhabitants to relocate to Shadyakh, its western suburb, over the next two decades.

But Hira cemetery was nowhere near the shrine to Muhammad Mahruq where Omar Khayyam's tomb has been thought, for several centuries now, to be located. The village of Hira, named for a pre-Islamic Arab city in Iraq, appears to have been settled by the Arabs who conquered Nishapur in the seventh century. It was located around the southeast corner of the walled city that defined pre-Islamic Nishapur and that is still easily visible both on the ground and in aerial photographs. Hira developed from a village into a prosperous urban quarter as the city expanded. It is likely that the city's main congregational mosque was located either within or close to Hira, judging from a report of a funeral ceremony in a contemporary biographical dictionary: "Along the main road he [the deceased] used to walk to the congregational mosque every Friday until it reached the prayer ground of al-Hira."[5]

Fortunately, the practice of visiting saintly tombs that gained increasing popularity after the eleventh century gave rise to tomb lists that guided pilgrims in their visitations. Four undated lists survive as addenda to a biographical dictionary of Nishapur that was compiled early in the eleventh century. The first and what is probably the oldest list begins by stating that certain companions of the Prophet were buried in northern Hira (*bala* = "upper" meaning upstream toward the mountains to the north of the city) in a spot also known as the cemetery of the Judge Nasr b. Ziyad. It also lists this spot, or one quite nearby, as the burial place of the great compiler of canonical *hadith* Muslim b. al-Hajjaj al-Qushairi (d. 875). This is what one would expect of a district dating to the time of the Arab conquest.

The next cemetery listed, Talajird, houses the shrine (*mashhad*) of Muhammad b. Muhammad b. Zaid b. Ali b. al-Husain b. Ali b. Abi Talib. This is Muhammad Mahruq, even though he is called a martyr (*shahid*) but not "the Burnt." The pious expressions accompanying this listing indicate that Shi'ism, or a least veneration of the family of Ali, had become popular by the time the list was compiled. Mention of an earthquake that struck Shadyakh in 1268 and the accompanying remark that no famous people were buried in Shadyakh after that event fit with this veneration. The existing shrine of

5. Al-Sam'ani, f446b. This reference is to the facsimile edition of al-Sam'ani, *Kitab al-ansab*, vol. XX of the E. J. Gibb Mermorial series, London, 1912. Cited in R. W. Bulliet, "Medieval Nishapur: A Topographic and Demographic Reconstruction," *Studia Islamica*, 5/1 (1976), 78.

Muhammad Mahruq on the western outskirts of the medieval city's ruins, close to the eastern wall of Shadyakh visible on aerial photographs, securely marks the location of the Talajird cemetery. It is a couple of kilometers west of Hira quarter.

The second list mentions only a handful of names, mostly Alids, starting with Muhammad b. Muhammad b. Zaid – still not called Mahruq – buried in Talajird cemetery. It also states that as a consequence of assaults and plundering, the pilgrimage sites had been obliterated and the tombs had disappeared so that no one any longer knew where the cemeteries were. The third list contains people's names, but no specifics as to where they were buried.

The final list, attributed to someone named Qutb al-Din begins by mentioning the tombs of the Prophet's companions in upper Hira and the location there of the cemetery of the Judge Nasr b. Ziyad. Then, seemingly for the same cemetery, it lists Muhammad Mahruq. After mentioning a few more worthies, it cites Muhammad b. Aslam al-Tusi, a semi-legendary ninth-century ascetic, as having his tomb "on the road to the shrine of Talajird," but does not associate the shrine with Muhammad Mahruq. Further along, it says of Muslim b. al-Hajjaj al-Qushairi, who was reported on the first list as being buried in Hira, that "his tomb in the tomb area (*turbabad*) east of the citadel is old." This rare mention of an actual compass point confirms the location of Hira and its associated cemeteries east of the pre-Islamic city, rather than way to the west where Muhammad Mahruq's shrine was and still is located. Several other cemeteries are named on this list only and probably refer to the places in Shadyakh where Nishapur was reincarnated.

There is no indication of when the list-maker Qutb al-Din lived, although his nickname Qutb al-Din and his referring to certain worthies as *javanmard* (meritorious "young man") and *alamdar* (illustrious "standard-bearer") might suggest the Safavid period, that is, the time when a major restoration of Muhammad Mahruq's shrine was undertaken. It seems apparent, however, that the waves of destruction that had eradicated local knowledge of the location of tombs worth visiting had opened the way to inventing new shrines and burial places. Though the place-name Talajird was still known, it was nowhere near as prominent historically as the district and cemetery of Hira.

My conjecture is that Qutb al-Din knew perfectly well that the shrine of Muhammad Mahruq was located in Talajird, but he arbitrarily identified it with the more famous Hira district. Inasmuch as the tombstone identifying Omar Khayyam's resting place in the same shrine is stylistically quite late, it may be that Qutb al-Din knew about the legend that he was buried in Hira and used that as the basis for renaming Talajird Hira. The real location of Hira had been lost even though the tomb of Muslim b. al-Hajjaj, which was definitely located in Hira, was still known to Qutb al-Din, and known to lie east of the citadel ... far, far away from Muhammad Mahruq's shrine.

Al-Husain the Blind

What a long shaggy dog story this has been! Who really cares who is buried where, so long as the tourists come to visit Khayyam's monument?

For me, this convoluted tale is of value because it helps explain the odd location of the peculiar ancient/modern tombstone of al-Husain the Blind: by the railroad tracks at the edge of a plowed field south-southeast of the pre-Islamic city and a couple of kilometers away from the shrine of Muhammad Mahruq. If a pious Nishapuri had experienced, as Dr. Modarressi has suggested, the blind son of the Prophet's great-great-grandson Zaid b. Ali beseeching him in a dream to sally forth and discover his long-lost resting place, why would the man have chosen that particular spot?

It is not in a cemetery, and at the time of its apparent (re)carving, it was too far from any road and too close to the tracks to be convenient for pious visitation. Wouldn't it have made more sense to "discover" the tomb in proximity to the shrine of Muhammad Mahruq, who was either al-Husain the Blind's son or his nephew? Then pilgrims could have showered it with blessings when they visited the resting place of his much more eminent descendant.

According to my topographic reconstruction, the spot where I encountered the strange stone fits quite well with the location of Hira quarter and its associated cemetery ... so long as we recognize that Omar Khayyam's historically attested burial in Hira was translocated, probably in Safavid times, to the district that had historically been known as Talajird.

Here I rest my case for the tombstone of al-Husain the Blind, despite its recent origin, being a true vestige of his last resting place. Someday, perhaps, this conjecture will be borne out by archaeological investigation and the good citizens of Nishapur will recover yet another vestige of their city's bygone glory.

THE WORLD

Isthmus Civilizations and the "Sapient Paradox"

(2014)

How Should We Define "Earliest Civilization"?

Caral, near the Pacific coast in northern Peru, flourished between 2600 and 2000 BCE. The main city of the Norte Chico culture that developed slightly earlier along the seacoast proper, Caral is the oldest known urban site in the Western Hemisphere. (I will henceforward refer to the Western Hemisphere as the New World, not because it was new to the Europeans in 1492 CE, but because it was new to human habitation during the last Ice Age. This newness plays a central role in the argument of this essay.) To build Caral's pyramids and other large structures, workers put stones in fiber bags and then placed the filled bags in the foundations and walls. The fibers provide plant remains suitable for precise carbon-14 analysis. Hence the firm dating of the site. About a thousand years elapsed between the disappearance of the Norte Chico culture and the formation of a more fully elaborated urban civilization in the Chavin culture in the Peruvian highlands. Meanwhile, a separate civilizational process bore fruit around 1500 BCE in southern Mexico in the form of the Olmec civilization.

In the Eastern Hemisphere, that is, in the Old World, Jericho, located in the valley of the Jordan River, is the oldest known urban site. It was inhabited as early as 9000 BCE and has been continuously occupied ever since. The somewhat later urban site of Çatal Hüyük in Turkey flourished between 7500 and 5700 BCE but was abandoned before the cultures that eventually developed into full-fledged urban civilizations in Egypt and Mesopotamia began to form around 5500–5000 BCE. The time interval between the founding of Jericho and Çatal Hüyük and the full development of the Pharaonic and Sumerian civilizations around 3100 BCE was four to six thousand years.

Like the people who lived in Caral, the earliest inhabitants of Jericho had not yet learned to make pottery, but they did grow and store wheat and barley. The people of Caral cultivated no grain at all. Their diet centered on domesticated squash, beans, and sweet potatoes. Their successors in Chavin, however, grew a grain-like staple known as quinoa, and their successors in turn, the Moche people, grew corn, which had been domesticated in Mexico far to the north and was already known to the Olmecs.

According to the conventional calculus of time that identifies the earliest archaeological sites and civilizations by counting backward from the present – BP=Before Present; BCE=Before the Common Era – there is no disagreement about the fact that the Old World holds the honor of hosting the earliest civilizations. Indeed, historians rarely discuss New World cultures when they are talking about the emergence of civilization in Egypt and Mesopotamia. And when they do, they tend to emphasize ways in which the peoples of the New World fell short of the civilizational model presented by the Old World, such as their lack of domestic animals and lack of wheeled transport. This despite the scholarly consensus that contacts between New and Old World civilizations were few and of minimal impact prior to the voyages of Columbus, which makes it logically impossible to postulate Old World civilizations as models for emulation by New World peoples.

According to an alternative calculus, one that counts forward instead of backward, this comparison between the Old and New Worlds should be reversed. Since no civilization could arise in any part of the world before that region became inhabited by modern humans (*homo sapiens sapiens*), it is possible to calculate the length of time between an area's first human habitation and the appearance there of civilized urban life. When the chronology of civilization is counted forward in this way, it becomes apparent that urban sites and civilizations developed much more rapidly in the New World than they did in the Old. Thus the New World civilizations may not have been the earliest in strict chronology, but they were certainly the earliest – perhaps most precocious would be a better term – in terms of the time it took people in Peru and southern Mexico to make the transition from palaeolithic foraging to urban settlement based on domesticated agriculture.

Though specific dates are subject to change in accordance with new archaeological and DNA analyses, the time of arrival of modern humans in Europe (Cro-Magnon man) and Australia is most often given as around 40,000 years ago. Though Egypt and the Near East were closer to the African homeland, where modern humans are believed to have first appeared around 50,000 years ago, the first migrants out of Africa seem to have followed the seacoasts from Africa, to southern Arabia, to Iran, to India, to Southeast Asia, to Australia before dispersing northward away from the seas. So prehistorians conjecture that the migration of modern humans to Egypt and the Near East may have taken 5000 years longer, being accomplished around 35,000 years ago.

The comparable date for the arrival of modern humans in the New World, according to traditional archaeological analysis, is seldom estimated to be more than 14,000 years ago, and the earliest evidence comes from

Canada and the United States rather than Mexico and South America.[1] Thus the span of time that separates the initial human habitation of the New World from the first site of urban civilization at Caral is roughly 13,400 years (14,000 BCE minus 2600 BCE), while the comparable span of time between the arrival of modern man in Egypt and the Near East and the first site of urban civilization at Jericho is more like 26,000 years (35,000 BCE minus 9000 BCE).

Table 1: Comparative Chronology of Earliest Civilizations

Time Before Common Era (BCE)	Eastern Hemisphere Old World	Western Hemisphere New World
900–200 BCE		Chavin culture in Peru
1500–400 BCE		Olmec culture in Mexico
2600–2000 BCE		Norte Chico culture (Caral) in Peru
5300–1940 BCE	Sumerian culture in Iraq	
5500–332 BCE	Ancient Egyptian culture	
9000 BCE	Jericho becomes an urban settlement	TIME GAP TO URBANISM 13,400 YEARS
14,000 BCE	TIME GAP TO URBANISM 26,000 YEARS	Modern humans reach the Americas
35,000 BCE	Modern humans reach Egypt and Near East	

A discrepancy of close to 13,000 years is no small matter, nor is the number likely to diminish in light of discoveries yet to be made. A popular overview of scientific opinion about human origins, Nicholas Wade's *Before the Dawn: Recovering the Lost History of our Ancestors*, cites the distinguished archaeologist Colin Renfrew in his discussion of the time lapse between the appearance of modern humans and of civilization:

1. There is an alternative theory based on carbon remains from rock shelters in the Pedra Furada district of the state of Piaui in northeastern Brazil that places human habitation as early as 40,000 BP, but there is no consensus among archaeologists on the validity of these claims, nor has there been any explanation of how people would have reached this location from Africa without leaving traces in intermediate Western Hemisphere locales. For the purposes of the argument presented in this essay, I will stick to the date of 14,000 BCE, especially since the Pedra Furada sites are far, far away from the points of origin of civilization in Peru and southern Mexico.

"If human societies of the early Upper Palaeolithic had this new capacity for innovation and creativity which notionally accompanies our species, why do we not hear more about them?" [Renfrew] asks. There is a 45,000-year delay between the time of the ancestral human population and the first great urban civilizations, such as those of Babylon, Egypt, the Harappan cultures of India and the Shang period of China. If "behaviorally modern" humans evolved 50,000 years ago, why did it take so long for this modernity to be put into practice? Renfrew calls this gap the "sapient paradox."[2]

The corollary question that must be addressed is why this supposed "sapient paradox" endured at least 13,000 years longer in the Old World than in the New?

Instead of dismissing New World civilizations as late, and consequently of less interest than those of, say, Egypt, Mesopotamia, the Indus Valley, and the North China plain, historians exploring the origin of civilization should be asking why the peoples of the New World were so precocious. Instead of trying to identify positive factors that contributed to the emergence of civilization in the Old World river valleys, historians should be more interested in considering whether in comparison to the New World, where civilization arose so much more quickly, there may have been factors that retarded the growth of civilization in the Old World. These might possibly include some of the same factors that have hitherto been considered goads to civilizational development, such as grain agriculture and the herding of animals.

It must be borne in mind that the people who managed to make the leap from Old Stone Age technology to civilization in Peru twice as fast as those who accomplished the same feat in the Nile Valley belonged to that same variant of humankind that is universally recognized to be a single undivided species everywhere in the world, *homo sapiens sapiens*. This severely limits any suggestion that the humans who are believed to have first reached the Americas already possessed certain cultural skills or outlooks that put them on a fast track to civilization. If, as is generally supposed, they arrived in the New World by migrating across the land bridge that opened up between Alaska and Siberia when the last Ice Age glaciation brought about dramatically lower world sea levels, their levels of culture and tool use upon entry should resemble those of their ancestors in northeast Asia. And in fact, the palaeolithic stone implements of the earliest humans in North America, those found at sites of the Clovis culture, are not substantially advanced be-

---

2. Nicholas Wade, *Before the Dawn: Recovering the Lost History of Our Ancestors*, (New York: The Penguin Press, 2006), 129.

yond their chronological counterparts in Europe and Asia.[3] Moreover, the northeast Asian or Siberian peoples most closely related to the migrants that crossed the Bering Strait land bridge, groups like the Chukchi and the Koryaks, retained a foraging lifestyle until modern times and never developed urban civilizations.

Given the high likelihood, therefore, that the palaeoindians who first inhabited the Americas had toolkits and cultural outlooks that differed little from those of their presumed ancestors in Siberia and Northeast Asia, it is reasonable to ask why they were so precocious in developing urban civilizations. The answer that will be posed here is that spatial constraints intrinsic to the geography of the Western Hemisphere, namely, the narrowness of the Mesoamerican isthmus and of the band of land between the Pacific coast and the high Andes, forced a development that did not have a parallel in the Old World until the desertification of the Sahara, Arabia, and Mesopotamia turned river valleys into isthmuses of green surrounded by minimally habitable deserts. In short, people developed civilization only when they ran out of room. The more expansive the space for dispersal, the longer the "sapient paradox." The rest of this essay will be devoted to elaborating this thesis.

Do Civilizations Begin in Temperate Lands or in the Tropics?

The words "tropic" and "tropical" connote exoticism, indolence, primitiveness, sensuality, and every manner of heat. These connotations differ only slightly from those associated with "the orient" and "oriental." However, they are not the products of imperialism as Edward Said has argued their Orientalist counterparts to be. Rather, they reflect the stereotypical views of the ancient Greeks and Persians. In dividing the world into five or seven climes (Gr. *klimata*, Pers. *keshvar*) thinkers like Aristotle declared the latitudinal bands nearest the equator to be too torrid for civilized habitation, and the lands near the poles to be too cold. Human civilization, they maintained, was appropriate to the temperate zones north and (for the ancients only theoretically) south of the tropics.

Later historiographical practice seldom challenged these perceptions. River valleys in the more temperate zones are still credited with hosting the world's first civilizations, and the torrid tropics with having climatic conditions that are antithetical to civilization, though the idea that the peoples of the tropics were burned black by the sun and thus rendered incapable of civilization has gone the way of most other blatantly racist theories. Today's

---

3. The fractured pebbles found at the Pedra Furada sites in Brazil are so rudimentary that many archaeologists doubt that they are human artifacts.

world history textbooks all ascribe the origins of civilization to the traditional Old World river valleys just north of the Tropic of Cancer.

In point of fact, however, as already demonstrated, the world's most precocious urban civilizations – as opposed to the chronologically earliest – appeared in the tropics of the New World, and the New World temperate zones in the United States and Argentina were latecomers to civilization. When the Olmecs, Mayans, and Aztecs were developing spectacular civilizations in tropical southern Mexico and Central America, and the Nazca, Wari, Chimú, Moche, and Incan peoples were flourishing in the tropical portion of South America between the Pacific coast and the peaks of the Andes, there was comparatively little going on in temperate North and South America.

The world historian Arnold Toynbee took note of this when he remarked:

> The most captious critic cannot deny that the environmental conditions offered by Egypt and Mesopotamia are also offered by the valleys of the Rio Grande and Colorado River in the United States. Under the hands of the modern European settler, equipped with resources he has brought with him from the other side of the Atlantic, these rivers of America have performed the miracles that the Nile and Euphrates performed for Egyptiac and Sumeric engineers. But this magic has never been taught by the Colorado or the Rio Grande to people who were not adepts at it already through having learnt it elsewhere.[4]

Unfortunately, the blatant invocation of European superiority and exceptionalism embodied in Toynbee's observation deprives it of the weight it might have borne if he had accompanied it with the opposite comparison of Mayan civilization in the rain forest tropics of Central America and the absence of any counterpart in the Congo. When both comparisons are made, the result is an intriguing mystery: Given that modern humans constitute one and the same species throughout the globe and that circumstances prompting or compelling people to create sophisticated urban civilizations have been experienced independently in a number of different places at a number of different times, is there any reason to believe with Aristotle that latitude is a crucial variable in this process? The most enduring Old World civilizations arose in more temperate climes, to be sure, but how can one conceive of proximity to the equator as a bar to civilizational development when the most impressive New World civilizations all arose in the tropics?

4. Arnold J. Toynbee, *A Study of History. Abridgement of Volumes I-VI by D. C. Somervell*, Oxford: Oxford University Press, 1947, vol. I, 58.

We cannot fault the Greeks and Persians for not being aware of what was happening on the other side of the globe, but we can certainly fault modern world historians for not drawing attention to the differences between the hemispheres and for repeating outworn stereotypes about the impossibility of civilization developing in the tropics. What is needed is a new approach to identifying the circumstances that gave rise to civilization.

Since the paradigmatic Old World civilizational pioneers, the Egyptians, the Mesopotamians, and the inhabitants of the Indus Valley, all lived in some degree of proximity to a major river and utilized riverine irrigation in growing their crops, historians have drawn an equation between civilization and the irrigated cultivation of grain crops in river valleys. This equation does not work in the New World, however. Though maize, a domestic plant derived from wild ancestors in Mexico and Nicaragua, eventually spread to become a staple food throughout the New World, a wealth of root crops, such as potatoes, manioc, and sweet potatoes; garden vegetables like beans, squash, and chili peppers; and tree fruits like avocado, cacao, and papaya provided rich and diverse diets in the New World tropics. In none of the early New World civilizations that have been studied has the cultivation of any of these crops been associated with river irrigation on a scale comparable to that found in Egypt, Mesopotamia, and the Indus Valley Civilization, though other sophisticated forms of irrigation, field preparation, and orchard planting were developed to increase production.

Conclusion: You don't need rivers to create a civilization. You don't need fields of grain irrigated by water from great rivers to create a civilization. You don't need a non-tropical climate to create a civilization.

How Did Foragers Live Before Civilization?

To find out what you do need for civilization I believe you must start with asking how people lived during the era of Renfrew's proposed "sapient paradox," the tens of thousands of foraging years that preceded, and then in many regions coexisted with, civilization. Then you must examine the ways scholars in various disciplines have imagined the processes by which bands of foragers, also known as hunter-gatherers but including fisher-folk and beachcombers, adopted lifeways that depended increasingly on cultivated plants. Dependence on cultivation is universally recognized as a sine qua non of civilization. The question of dependence on domestic animals must also be addressed, but it is largely peripheral to a general concern with the origins of civilization since no domestic animal played a major role in the most precocious civilizations of the New World.

The population density that can be sustained by foraging obviously differs from one environment to another. Fish and mollusks can satisfy the protein needs of seashore, lakeshore, or riverbank groups without requiring them to disperse to avoid overhunting. The fish make themselves available to human predation of their own accord. But this does not relieve the fisher folk of the need to forage for edible plants, unless they have adapted to almost complete dependence on animal protein and fat. As for the gathering of wild fruits, roots, and berries, a tropical rain forest will provide more opportunities than a grassy steppe or a rocky desert. So human population densities must have varied with their habitats.

This means there is no easy way to determine the average population of forager bands before the rise of civilization. That being said, population density estimates made on the basis of archaeology and studies of foraging groups in the nineteenth and twentieth centuries may not be far off the mark. Thus it may not be unreasonable to guess that the groups that witnessed the rise of the first civilizations in various parts of the world descended from bands of foragers that averaged 50 to 150 members, or one per square mile in an area with a radius of between four and seven miles.

If that number is wrong, it may not make much difference. The crucial consideration is that in the absence of some sort of cultivation or planting of fruit-bearing trees, there was no way to increase dramatically the available quantity of edible plants. To be sure, a group could develop more efficient means of hunting and fishing as they did with the bow-and-arrow and fishing hook, and they could devise ways to make the inedible edible, as they did when they discovered techniques for removing or neutralizing the poisonous juices of the cassava (manioc) plant. But there were limits to how far such improvements could proceed in terms of increasing the number of calories available per person.

The consequence of this situation, as every prehistorian has realized, is that beyond a certain point, unrestrained population growth would necessarily threaten the livelihood of the forager group. For Nicholas Wade, "an existence dominated by incessant warfare" conveniently explains how foragers kept their populations in check.[5] But this is only an assumption, though one that is shared by the likes of Steven Pinker in *The Better Angels of Our Nature* (2014).[6] Physical evidence of endemic warfare between groups fighting to protect their foraging areas in the era before civilization is hard to come by. Another theory maintains that growing numbers of mouths to feed led to the deliberate planting, and thus the domestication, of selected food plants.

5. Wade, *Before the Dawn*, 9.
6. Stephen Pinker, *The Better Angels of Our Nature: Why Violence Has Declined*, New York: Viking, 2011.

Agriculture could indeed sustain higher population densities than foraging. Ironically, however, the evidence for warfare among early groups engaged in crop growing is far more abundant than among foragers.

The problem with the theory that increasing numbers in and of themselves prompted experiments with growing and storing food plants is that the foraging manner of life continued for tens of thousands of years without hitting the limit of population growth that would trigger a shift to agriculture. And in some habitats the foraging lifestyle evolved a sufficient balance between population and the carrying capacity of the environment to survive down to the twentieth century without agriculture.

Was there a natural equilibrium in pre-agricultural societies that kept population more or less constant? If so, why and how did it break down? Alternatively, was population growth among foraging groups somehow accommodated without changing the balance between population density and the natural carrying capacity of the environment? If so, why did this accommodation cease functioning?

Exploration of the first possibility, that long-standing restraints on population growth somehow broke down, leads, on the one hand, to questions about changes in the incidence of death by misadventure, principally being killed in war or by predators, and/or infanticide or other measures groups might have taken to limit the number of mouths they had to feed. On the other hand, it ascribes the breakdown of population limits to the greater abundance of food made possible by developing and cultivating domestic crops.

Either of these two alternatives leads to problems. If humans stopped waging war at a level sufficient to check population growth, or learned to escape or ward off their predators, or turned away from practices like infanticide to such a degree that foraging groups grew too big to live on what they could gather or obtain by hunting and fishing, why did that happen around ten thousand years ago in the Old World and, independently, perhaps six thousand years ago in the New World? A climatic warming brought about by the waning of the last Ice Age, the end of the so-called Younger Dryas period, is the usual answer for the Old World, but it doesn't work very well for the New. There are even indications that deglaciation may have begun a thousand years earlier in South America than in the Northern Hemisphere with the postulated Huelmo/Mascardi Cold Reversal. But the return of the warming sun did not immediately stir people in Peru and Mesoamerica to breed more children and domesticate plants in the way that students of the Neolithic revolution in the Old World have postulated. In other words, while climate change seems plausible as an explanation for domestication in the Old World, it has little to offer in studying the New. Yet the New World peoples were thousands of years more precocious in their achievement of civilization.

The other option, that population growth was somehow naturally accommodated until it wasn't, and that that point was reached far more rapidly in the New World, relative to the initial arrival there of humankind, than in the Old, leads to a chicken-or-egg conundrum. Premise: cultivated plants make for greater population densities because they increase the number of calories per acre. Alternative premise: growing population prompts foraging groups to experiment with cultivation, even though tens of thousands of years of adaptation to their environments had not previously led them to imagine that plants could or needed to be deliberately cultivated. One can make a superficially sensible argument starting with either premise, but logically speaking, one or the other must have come first. Complicating this conundrum are concrete indications that in the Old World, civilized populations supported by cultivated crops often (or usually?) had worse health, poorer nutrition, and more rotten teeth than the foraging groups they supplanted. New World domesticated plants seem to have provided more balanced nutrition.

Why Did Human Foragers Disperse Around the World?

It will prove worthwhile to explore an alternative to these lines of speculation, to wit, that population growth among foraging groups was accommodated by the movement of surplus population into uninhabited territory, and that the pressures that resulted in the domestication of plants, and thus subsequently in the emergence of civilization, came to be felt when there was no accessible unoccupied territory to move to. The operative factor in this hypothesis is a view of the foraging lifestyle that assumes an innate human preference for avoiding conflict, including warfare, by seeking separation from other people.

The original homeland of hominid development was in East Africa, where it is reasonable to assume that the coevolution of prey species and predator species initially operated as a check on hominid overpopulation, just as foxes balance out snowshoe rabbits in Canada and lions cull the herds of herbivores on the Serengeti Plain. Punctures in some early hominid skulls roughly match the dentition of leopards, which has prompted the suggestion that these big cats dragged our earliest ancestors into trees to consume them at their leisure. Once early hominids developed bipedalism and forsook the forest for savannah grasslands, however, they must have become prey for other species. Hyenas make a better candidate than lions because they are closer to hominids in size and down to recent times make a practice of building dens close to human settlements. Also, since hyenas eat bones as well as soft tissue, a habit that renders their feces white with calcium, they would have left few human skeletons for today's archaeologists to find.

Regardless of who ate our early ancestors, however, there was ample time, at least 700,000 years, between the appearance of the first hominid tool users (*homo habilis* – 2.5 million years ago) and the first evidence of hominid migration out of Africa (*homo georgicus* – 1.8 million years ago) for any imbalances in predator-prey relationships associated with the change of habitat from forest to savannah to correct themselves. Then another 1.6 million years elapsed before *homo sapiens sapiens*, modern humans, come into evidence in East African fossil assemblages. Again, it is reasonable to assume that at every new stage of development our ancestors, who were comparatively weak animals despite being increasingly able to defend themselves with primitive stone weapons and firebrands, suffered from regular predation by large carnivores that were coadapting to the same changes in climate and habitat. Indeed, there is nothing to suggest that *homo erectus*, the first hominid species to appear in multiple non-African habitats as far apart as Europe, China, and Indonesia, produced large populations.

This assumption of predator-prey equilibrium becomes less plausible, however, once modern humans began to disperse from their African homeland. First appearing in East Africa around 200,000 years ago, modern humans show up in Australia by 40,000 BCE, presumably having migrated along the seacoasts. They reach Europe, largely ice-covered during the Würm glaciation, at about the same time. And they are in evidence in Egypt and the Near East at least by 35,000 BCE. Though these time spans are substantial and subject to change with new archaeological discoveries, there is no question but that modern humans encountered and adapted to scores of different habitats during these several tens of thousands of years. With their large brains and ever more effective tools, they were increasingly able to kill whatever animals they encountered. Some they ate; others they killed to avoid being eaten. But no coevolving carnivore with an established taste for human flesh migrated with them from Africa, and the beasts they encountered in their migrations did not necessarily look upon humans as prey. Other factors contributing to mortality being constant – which, of course, they couldn't have been – this situation alone should have led to increased survival, and consequently population growth.

From the point of view of Colin Renfrew's "sapient paradox," it is reasonable to ask whether learning how to survive in new habitats populated by strange plants and animals was in any way a lesser cognitive challenge to *homo sapiens sapiens'* "innate capacity for innovation and creativity" than learning how to build a stone house or plant a crop.

Are Modern Humans a Domestic Species?

Before proceeding further, consideration should be given to the question of domestication. Though there is no agreed-upon definition of the word "domestic" as applied to animals, "wild" is generally taken as its antonym. Human intervention in breeding; human utilization of the flesh and products of domestic animals, including their labor; and genetic changes directly or indirectly caused by association with human populations are among the elements taken into account in different definitions. However, one constant that is common to all definitions, but seldom accorded much attention, is the fact that domestic animal populations are normally removed or protected from the predator-prey relationships of their wild ancestors and cousins. Migrating humans remove their animals physically from habitats where they have coevolved as prey for specific carnivorous species. And at the same time, they protect them by killing or chasing off whatever predators they encounter, either old or new.

Insofar as predation plays a role in keeping animal populations in balance with the carrying capacity of their habitats, human removal or protection of domestic animals from their natural predation environment should increase their rate of population growth. This expectation accords with reality. Domestic breeds have reproduced far more abundantly than their wild counterparts over the centuries, to the extent that many of their wild ancestors, such as the aurochs, the ancestor of domestic cattle, and the wild one-humped camel, have become extinct. Moreover, when domestic populations are brought to new regions, the local predators, which have coevolved in balance with the local prey species, may pay too little attention to them to keep them from exceeding the carrying capacity of the region. When the Spaniards brought sheep to northern Mexico, for example, the presence of indigenous pumas, wolves, and coyotes did not prevent the sheep from multiplying so rapidly that they eventually overgrazed the land and experienced a massive famine-induced die-off.[7] In fact, imported domestic animals have not infrequently become so numerous as to be considered vermin. These include rabbits and camels in Australia, pigs and goats on any number of remote islands, and pigeons, the feral versions of domesticated European rock doves, everywhere in the world.

---

7. This episode is documented in great detail in Elinor G. K. Melville, *A Plague of Sheep: Environmental Consequences of the Conquest of Mexico* (Cambridge: Cambridge University Press, 1997).

Looking at modern humans from this perspective, it is tempting to think that the reason they became so numerous while other hominids went extinct is precisely because they migrated so far away from the hyenas, wild dogs, and lions of their homeland, and because they developed more and more effective ways to kill whatever new predators they encountered, like the saber-toothed cats that were still roaming the New World when they arrived.[8] Thus they benefited from precisely the aspects of human activity that their domestic herds and flocks were later to benefit from. That is to say, the impulse to occupy lands not previously known to humankind amounted to an unconscious form of self-domestication. As their numbers grew, their migrations expanded, and they became increasingly oriented toward personal and group survival and less accepting of violent death in the jaws of a predator as a natural end-of-life scenario.

What Did Modern Humans Eat When They Moved into New Territories?

In most natural environments the number of plant species that humans can safely eat and digest represents a quite small subset of all plant life. Cellulose, which is abundantly available in wood and grasses, is so indigestible that the great herds of animals that live by grassland grazing rely on microorganisms in their gut to break it into more absorbable compounds. Even the nutritious and digestible portions of plants may contain poisonous or noxious substances that have to be removed before the plants become edible. This applies to a wide range of domesticated plants including cassava, taro, and cashew nuts. Certain other plants, like rhubarb, may have poisonous leaves but edible stems. Studies of ethnobotany around the world tell us that local foraging populations accumulate massive bodies of expert lore identifying which local species may be eaten or used for medical purposes and which may not. This lore is often lost when civilized folk dependent on domestic plants replace the foragers. One might look upon this as a reverse "sapient paradox," that is, a systematic loss of knowledge resulting from the application of innovation and creativity to the works of civilization.

When prehistoric foraging groups moved from one habitat to another and found themselves confronted by many unfamiliar plants, the lore relat-

8. Proponents of the theory of megafaunal extinction, according to which humans willfully exterminated all large New World species, rely on the supposition that animals that did not coevolve with hominids did not instinctively run from the newcomers and thus became easy prey. While flight from humans may indeed have been rare when humans first appeared – even today Pampas deer and guanacos in Argentina don't flee human hunters – it is hard to imagine that top carnivores like the saber-toothed cats stood around passively when humans approached armed with stone axes.

ing to their home area could have been only partially transferrable to the new. Teff, for example, a grass with tiny edible seeds found in the Ethiopian highlands that were part of the African homeland of modern humans, would not have been found in India, China, or Canada. Hence, the hominids that migrated out of East Africa – whether *homo erectus*, or *homo sapiens neanderthalensis*, or *homo sapiens sapiens* – to lands previously uninhabited by humans would have been in grave danger of poisoning or starvation during the period of time, more likely years rather than months, that it would have taken them to acquire, by trial and error, an inventory of the edible plants, plant parts, and processing requirements of the new array of flora they encountered in their new habitat. This makes it unlikely that in their migration era they depended exclusively or primarily on plants for sustenance.

What made it possible, then, for humans to migrate to all habitable parts of the globe when the change from one ecozone to another must have involved such risk to their vegetational sustenance? The short answer to this question is meat. Unlike plants, which have evolved all sorts of defenses to fend off being eaten by animals, animal flesh is mostly edible. East African migrants arriving in India would not have found any elands, but they could eat the local nilgai with no toxic effect, just as those arriving in Europe could eat the previously unfamiliar horses and bison they encountered, or those arriving in Arctic North America could eat the seals and walruses. In each environment, it is reasonable to suppose that the first human migrants survived largely on the flesh of animals they killed, fished for, or scavenged while they slowly, and probably painfully, learned about the unfamiliar flora they encountered. This could explain both the posited exterminations of large animals in new lands like Australia and North America, if these actually occurred, and a subsequent shift away from hunting and fishing as immigrant groups slowly learned what plants they could eat and how to prepare them safely.

Underlying this supposition is the idea that the movement of hominids out of Africa depended upon the prior adoption of an at least partially carnivorous diet and the fabrication of tools that could be used for hunting, butchering, and fishing. Had these hominids still been herbivores, they would have followed the pattern of other herbivores and remained in their home habitat where they already knew what was on the menu. Even meat-eaters have territorial restrictions, of course, depending on the range of the prey species they have coevolved with. Thus polar bears live where there are seals and anteaters where there are ants and termites. But once our ancestors developed a taste for flesh and the means to kill whatever they wanted to kill, the world was their oyster.

How Did Social Relations Contribute to Expansion out of Africa?

A corollary notion relates to the highly plausible and widespread assumption that males have always played a greater role in hunting than females. Studies of foraging societies that survived down to modern times often describe ways of equitably distributing a successful hunter's game:

> Egalitarian hunter-gatherers have developed a variety of ways to level individuals.... Humor is used to belittle the successful hunter ... and gambling, accusations of stinginess, or demand sharing maintain a constant circulation of goods and prevent hoarding.... The hunter who acknowledges his worthlessness while dropping a fat antelope by the hearth relieves the tension created by sharing.[9]

Male hunters may not always have serviced groups of foragers, however. One problem with thinking that early hominid life, from *homo erectus* to *homo sapiens sapiens*, is best understood through comparison with small, homogeneous, cooperative groups of primates (usually chimpanzees) is that the comparison makes it hard to explain how humans came to populate the world. Why should small-group sociability have stimulated early bands of foragers to depart from congenial environments and wander off into possibly uncongenial ones? Wanderlust? Adventure? Hardly. Humans today do evolve group behaviors, but only rarely do they head off in entirely new directions except under extreme duress.

Possibly there was a time in human history when males who had not, or could not, establish themselves in breeding groups found the company of other male humans so undesirable that they deliberately distanced themselves from other individuals and groups. Male orangutans living solitary jungle lives provide a plausible example. Let us call this self-isolating attitude *monachophilia*, "the love of being alone." It is likely that the first person to hike into the Yosemite valley, or contemplate Niagara Falls, or see Ayers Rock was a single male who didn't like being around other people and didn't care much whether anyone else followed his wandering footsteps. A scenario in which these adventures into the unknown were carried out by human bands that included women and children is hard to imagine. Pioneer settlers may well travel in groups, but they are preceded by socially isolated frontiersmen who smell bad, behave unacceptably, and are nearly inarticulate.

Every pre-modern culture harbors a special regard for hermits, yogis on mountaintops, silent monks, and poorly socialized thinkers and artists.

9. Robert K . Kelly, *The Foraging Spectrum: Diversity in Hunter-Gatherer Lifeways* (Washington: Smithsonian Institution Press, 1995), 296.

New discoveries, techniques of meditation, visions of God, and so forth are more often than not attributed to socially isolated male monachophiles who today are often demeaned as loners, outsiders, or sociopaths. Wise women, by contrast, are usually visualized as playing key roles in the preservation of the group and of the group's store of knowledge and skills.

Once the foraging bands, followed by civilized settlers, filled up the world's empty spaces and closed the frontiers, however, they turned on the monachophiles because they did not know how to socialize. All that is left today is the male retiree who longs to sail the Atlantic by himself, or to estivate in his cabin in the mountains, or to hike the Appalachian Trail alone. We still have our share of monachophiles living in society, if course, but we encourage them to get help and learn how to fit in. We don't have enough margins left for them to dwell in.

How different were we 20,000 years ago? Given the hypothesis cited earlier of incessant warfare among foraging groups seeking to defend a home region, it is hard to see why the members of the group most capable of fighting on its behalf, namely, the hunters, would have chosen to wander into unknown territory if it was truly in their nature to defend their hearth? To be sure, it might be supposed that the initial dispersal of humans around the globe came at the hands of losers who failed to protect their territory and had to slink off into the wastes. But why would anyone follow them? Monachophilia as an inborn instinct coded in some small segment of male DNA offers a plausible alternative.

Be that as it may, in the absence of convincing evidence that pre-civilizational foraging amounted to constant warfare, it might alternatively be supposed that when a foraging group sensed a conflict-threatening encroachment by neighbors, the group preferred to strike out for unoccupied territory, previously explored by male monachophiles, rather than fight to the death to hold onto their existing domain. Down to the present day, males often entertain fantasies of trekking through the wild, living off the land, and proving their manhood by battling the elements and wild predators. Far less often do they dream of smashing enemy warriors in the face with axes or toiling in the fields seven days a week to produce a harvest of wheat.

What Constraints Did Humans Face in Their Dispersal?

So this brings us to the hinge point in the argument for an isthmus conjecture concerning the origins of urban civilization. If male hunters and fishers, particularly those of monachophilic tendencies, preferred venturing into new lands to fighting for dominance over old ones, what would have happened when there was no more space for them to move into?

This question takes on special significance when one looks at the geographical regions where unoccupied land was most likely to have become scarce. In latitudinal terms, the Old World tropics are incredibly spacious. Africa is at its widest between the equator and the Tropic of Cancer. Things look more constrained further east in Asia, but when the world's seas were 400 feet shallower during the last Ice Age, mainland and island southeast Asia constituted a single landmass comparable to Europe in size. Scholars refer to this landmass as Sunda and note that it was separated by only a narrow strait from a combined Australia-New Guinea continent-size landmass, which they call Sahul. India was not as spacious as those other two regions, but it was still a broad land in the north.

The contrast with the New World tropics is striking. Most of the land area between the equator and the Tropic of Cancer is taken up by the narrow isthmus of Central America as far north as central Mexico. Nor was there much more land area during the Ice Age that brought humans into the New World. The Pacific Ocean becomes very deep just off shore in both North and South America. Mexico's Yucatan peninsula extended northeastward into the Caribbean, though not as far as Cuba, but Central America added only a modest amount of territory. Northeastern South America gained a larger expanse of land, but the northeast was not, by current understandings, where South American civilization first developed. That distinction belongs to the narrow belt of land that is geographically constrained between the Pacific Ocean and the soaring Andes, which was scarcely more spacious during the Ice Age than it is today, or perhaps even less so since the southern Andes were topped by glaciers. It is also worth noting that the Pacific coast of the Americas is almost devoid of nearby islands, and the islands of the Caribbean, though close to northeastern South America during the Ice Age, were too far from Mexico and Central America to have been easily reached, or perhaps even known, in palaeolithic times.

Looking at the spacious tropics of the Old World during the last Ice Age and the narrowly constrained tropics of the New World in terms of the room available for foraging groups to strike off into unoccupied lands, there can be no question that tropical Africa, India, Southeast Asia (Sunda), and Australia (Sahul) were vastly more commodious. Looking at the same comparison from the standpoint of the geographical origin of civilizations, there can be no question that the commodious Old World tropics developed later than the corresponding temperate zones to their north while the geographically constrained New World tropics developed earlier than the corresponding temperate zones both to the north and the south.

The scenario this comparison suggests is the following: Foraging groups worldwide tended to retreat from conflict situations caused by population pressure. Led by male hunters and fishers, they set off for uninhabited territory and in so doing established a very broad extension of very low-density human settlement, eventually producing a scattering of people in almost every habitable part of the globe. But at some point in time, in certain areas, space ran out. With no place to move to without encroaching on groups that had already established themselves, individuals who would previously have been exploring new frontiers were unable to avoid conflict ... or at least collaboration. Conflict had two outcomes: social stratification, with some individuals achieving dominance over others; and greater population density as provision was found, albeit at lower nutritional levels, for the subordinated individuals who had not been able to move away. As for collaboration, that is what may be presumed by the emergence of farming, an activity that cannot take place without a modicum of cooperation and exchange.

How Does Plant Domestication Relate to Civilization?

This scenario suggests that a crucial factor in increasing population density, namely, the development of more reliable and abundant sources of food, involved the shrinkage of access to unoccupied lands. Where land was constrained, as in southern Mexico, Central America, and Peru, coping with an increasing density of population laid the groundwork for the eventual emergence of civilized life. That is to say, domestication of plants and the discovery of processes for making the inedible edible set these regions on a path of increasing population density that eventually led to urban civilization. By contrast, where land was essentially unlimited, as in tropical Africa and Australia, population dispersal though migration to new lands relieved the pressures that in Belize and Peru conduced toward civilization. In Southeast Asia, which gradually became spatially constrained as sea levels rose, population dispersal took the form of migration to islands that had once been part of the Sunda mainland. The history of sail design strongly suggests that sailing canoes intended for human migration, as opposed to trade, originated in the Sunda region.

Yet too much emphasis should not be placed on the process of plant domestication. Many plants were domesticated in regions that never developed the type of urbanism witnessed in Egypt, Mesopotamia, the Andes, or Mexico. Though plant origins are not easy to determine, archaeological studies indicate that bananas, yams, and taro (colocasia) were deliberately cultivated in mounds and processed at Kuk Swamp in New Guinea by 6500 years ago, and possibly earlier. But there was no subsequent development of urban civilization based on the increase in calorie production per acre that these valuable staples should have made possible. Likewise, in tropical Africa, yams, teff, and pearl millet seem all to have been domesticated before the appearance of urban civilization in Egypt and the Mesopotamia, but without giving rise to similar civilizations. And in the New World, manioc (cassava), an enormously important staple, appears to have been domesticated in southern Brazil, possibly as early as 8000 BCE. Yet southern Brazil never developed an urban civilization in pre-Columbian times even though manioc spread to more northerly regions and to the Caribbean islands where it became an essential food for early societies.

Two reasonable conclusions may be drawn from these examples. First, both the New World and the Old World tropics have such great biodiversity that there are numerous plant species suitable for domestication. Secondly, domesticating plants does not necessarily lead to urban civilization. Nevertheless, domestication does lead to increased yields in calories per acre and thus a reduced need for foraging and a higher carrying capacity for human population. What this suggests with regard to the origins of civilization is that plant domestication is a necessary but not a sufficient component.

How Does the Isthmus Principle Apply to Old-World Civilizations?

If civilizations came into being when people ran out of space, whether they were foraging groups or sedentary villagers who were trying to cope with greater numbers by experimenting with farming, then the crucial moment in the Old World would have been, as archaeologists have long maintained, the era of increasing aridity and desertification that began to afflict the Sahara, the Arabian peninsula, Mesopotamia, and southern Iran around 5000 BCE. This was a slow process with maximum aridity in Egypt being reached around 2500 BCE. Throughout this broad region deserts expanded and remnant lakes dried up. The Nile, Tigris, Euphrates, and Indus valleys became ribbons of green walled in by uninhabitable wastes.

Someone living in the Nile Valley might try migrating to the already populated lands to the north or south, but not into the deserts to the east or the west that desertification had emptied of people. Tributary streams that drained into the Nile from the bordering lands gradually dried up and the valley narrowed to just a couple of miles with a few habitable outlying oases where fossil ground water could still be found. The division of the valley into competing regions, called nomes, and then into northern and southern kingdoms, before its unification under a single pharaoh, supports this interpretation. Limitations of space forced people into more and more intense patterns of stratification and centralized authority.

In Mesopotamia, the desert to the west of the Euphrates became just about as arid as the deserts of Egypt. Yet this is the direction that migrants came from. People speaking Semitic languages left the increasingly arid borderlands and entered the space controlled by the Sumerian city-states. Eventually they became the dominant population, and the city-states, like the nomes of Egypt, became engulfed in larger states and eventually empires. Southern Iraq bordering the torrid and increasingly arid Arabian Peninsula was much more affected by these early migrants than northern Iraq, particularly near the Taurus Mountains, where the climate did not deteriorate so catastrophically. As for the Tigris, the plain separating the arable river lands from the Zagros Mountains became arid like the rest of lowland Iraq, but it was not very wide. So immigration from the east is less apparent in the historical record than the appearance of Semitic-speaking peoples challenging for living space from the west. Eventually, invaders like the Kassites and Persians did come from the east, but they were mountain dwellers and arrived more as conquerors than as participants in folk migrations.

The same isthmus principle can be applied to the Indus Valley in Pakistan. The era of desertification that produced the Saharan, Arabian, and Syrian deserts afflicted the regions east of the Persian Gulf, that is, the coastal Makran region of southern Iran, which was later a torture for Alexander's army to march through, and the Baluchistan coastal region of southeastern Iran and southwestern Pakistan, with similar dryness. The one great river that drained the mountains of Afghanistan and northern Pakistan was the Indus, which flowed through an increasingly arid landscape. It became the site of a major urban civilization. One lesser river, the Helmand, flowed out of Afghanistan into the Iranian desert. It produced one known urban site going back to the era of the Sumerians and the Indus Valley Civilization. This site, Shahra-e Sokhteh, was more like Çatal Hüyük, Göbekli Tepe, or Jericho insofar as it did not become the nucleus of a long-lasting civilization.

To summarize, the notion of isthmus civilizations is predicated on the assumption that prehistoric human foragers preferred migration to conflict. As their numbers expanded, they spread out. When their numbers continued to expand, they intensified their exploitation of local food resources by domesticating some species and devising processing techniques to maximize the use of others. When population expanded still more and there was nowhere left to move to, conflict was inevitable, and with conflict came the dominance of some groups over others, accumulation of property by the dominant groups, and a division of labor to produce the array of consumption items desired by the dominant groups. In short, civilization.

According to this conjecture, it was natural for plant domestication to substantially precede civilization, and for episodes of domestication in commodious lands, such as the Old World tropics or the Amazon basin in Brazil, not to lead to urban civilizations. Urbanism only came about when space was severely constrained with respect of population density. And because the New World tropics in southern Mexico, Central America, and the Pacific coastal regions of northwest South America were the most geographically constrained areas in the world, that is where civilizations exhibited the most precocious development.

In the Old World, to be sure, urban civilization emerged at a chronologically earlier point. But foraging and early farming villages afforded an adequate array of living patterns, relative to population density, until the severe desertification that began around 5000 BCE and created the functional equivalent of isthmuses in the form of great rivers flowing through deserts. The peoples who had foraged or planted crops in the lands that were becoming too dry for habitation had nowhere to move to except the river valleys. The Old World tropics south of the Tropic of Cancer, however, remained spacious enough to make civilization unnecessary. So the world's earliest, though not most precocious, urban civilizations came into being in the Old World river valley isthmuses of the desiccated temperate zone north of the Tropic of Cancer.

With respect to Colin Renfrew's idea that the long delay between the first emergence of modern humans and the beginnings of urban civilization constitutes a "sapient paradox," an alternative conjecture would suggest that civilization wasn't seen at the time as such a wonderful feat, or one that called for great innovation and creativity. It was a system of oppression generated by the need to cope with the absence of space to relieve growing population densities. It must be kept in mind that the people who pioneered urban civilization could have had no idea what their new way of life might lead to. The isthmus conjecture suggests that civilizations came about primarily because other ways of accommodating growing populations had been exhausted. In civilized society, the elite worked little and ate well while the great majority toiled to the point of exhaustion and retained only enough of their harvests to stay alive. This as opposed to the more egalitarian distribution of food and superior nutrition that seem to have been enjoyed by those foragers who were able to maintain, in large part through continual exploitation of new lands, a balance between population and the carrying capacity of their habitats. The works of civilization were indeed innovative and creative, particularly from an archaeological perspective focusing on built environments, but no more so than the accomplishments of foragers. Egyptians, Sumerians, and Harappans in the Indus Valley, for example, learned how to make bricks and build buildings, but the pre-civilizational foragers of the New World discovered dozens of varieties of halucinogenic cactus. It is hard to state definitively that the former achievement shows greater innovation and creativity than the latter.

What About the Fish?

Jericho was on the Jordan River, Çatal Hüyük on the Çarsamba River, Shahr-e Sukhteh on the Helmand River. Other important proto-urban sites in Bulgaria, Romania, and Ukraine were on the Danube, the Pruth, and other rivers draining the Carpathian and Balkan mountains. All of these communities grew wheat and barley, but none of them took the next step to a full-fledged urban civilization. The isthmus conjecture offers a simple explanation for the pre-Sumerian and pre-Pharaonic cultures of what Marija Gimbutas has labeled Old Europe not reaching the threshold of urban civilization. There was plenty of space in Turkey and Southeast Europe for people to respond to population pressure by dispersing. As David W. Anthony explains in his survey of the archaeology of Southeast Europe:

> Between about 4200 and 3900 BCE more than six hundred tell settlements [i.e. village occupation sites] ... were burned and abandoned in the lower Danube valley and eastern Bulgaria ... People scattered and became much more mobile, depending for their food on herds of sheep and cattle rather than fixed fields of grain.[10]

This option was not available in Egypt and Mesopotamia because the neighboring countryside was too arid to support extensive herds. It was not available in the Jordan valley either. Desert encroaches on both the western and the eastern banks of the river. So perhaps there was an additional reason for people being drawn to settle beside the big rivers: the Nile, Euphrates, Tigris, and Indus. If so, the most likely attraction was fish.

Fishbones are generally too small and too perishable to show up in archaeological surveys, but another way of estimating a prehistoric culture's consumption of fish has recently been developed. Nitrogen has two stable isotopes, nitrogen-14 and nitrogen-15. Both are found in plant and animal remains recovered from archaeological sites. They are not found in equal proportions, however. Animal bones have a markedly higher level of nitrogen-15 than plant tissues, and fish have a markedly higher level of nitrogen-15 than terrestrial animals, unless the latter are fish eaters, like bears and humans. It seems that animals excrete nitrogen-14 more readily

---

10. David W. Anthony, *The Horse, the Wheel, and Language* (Princeton: Princeton University Press, 2007), 227.

than nitrogen-15, so the more meat an animal has in its diet, the more the latter isotope accumulates. Carnivores have higher levels if they consume other carnivores, as is common with fish, than if they eat herbivores. Consequently, a comparison of the level of nitrogen-15 in human bones and in the bones of herbivores like cattle and sheep from the same site can signal the importance of fish in the human diet. The higher the human level relative to the herbivore level, the more fish in the diet.

Since isotopic analysis of nitrogen is a relatively new procedure and other environmental processes, such as desertification, can also affect animal nitrogen levels, the results available to a world historian who is neither an archaeologist nor a scientist are more suggestive than conclusive. For example, a finding that 7000–5000-year-old mummies preserved at Chinchorro in the Atacama desert of northern Chile near the Peruvian border have nitrogen-15 levels indicating that ninety-five percent of their protein consumption came from the sea seems appropriate.[11] The cold, upwelling Humboldt Current that hugs the coast of northern Chile and Peru is the world's most productive marine ecosystem. Thus the nitrogen-15 analysis confirms the common-sense assumption that it was a superabundance of fish that attracted people to this arid coast, where Caral became the first major urban site, and helped stimulate the development of civilization in an otherwise inhospitable region.

On the other hand, it may come as a surprise to learn that the settled peoples of Old Europe, who practiced grain agriculture and herded cattle, sheep, and goats, just like the Egyptians and Sumerians, had a diet in which half of their animal protein came from fish.[12] Standard accounts of the birth of urban civilization in the Old World scarcely mention fish and certainly pay less attention to fishing than to grain growing and herding. Yet as one reflects on the fish factor, a different way of looking at the beginning of the Egyptian and Mesopotamian civilizations emerges. If the early peoples living in the comparatively temperate and rain blessed regions north of the Black Sea obtained half of their animal protein by fishing in the region's numerous rivers, their contemporaries in Egypt and Mesopotamia probably consumed an equivalent – more likely a larger – proportion from the great rivers flowing through their deserts. Indeed, with growing aridity, and probably overhunting, reducing the availability of game, moving to the banks of the rivers to take advantage of their fish may have become more and more appealing. But this would only be true of big rivers. Smaller streams, like the

11. Sierra Bellows, "Hair Detective," The University of Virginia Magazine, on-line at uvamagazine.org/features/article/the_hair_detective/, retrieved August 26, 2011.

12. Anthony, *Horse*, 127, 175–6, 467–70.

Jordan or Çarsamba or Helmand, would not have had enough fish to support large populations. This is only a conjecture, of course, but it helps explain why big rivers flanked by deserts provided environments suitable to the development of urban civilizations while small rivers did not, even when they flowed through lands that were hospitable to grain farming and herding.

What About Wheat and Barley?

European and American historians are the descendants of people whose daily sustenance, literally their daily bread, was based on cereal grains. This instills in them an unconscious bias in favor of seeing bread (or pasta) as the staff of life, and the cultivation of the grain needed to make these products as the basis of civilized life. Yet corn and soy beans, neither of which has a history in Europe prior to 1500 CE, each account for twice as much farm acreage as wheat in the United States today, and barley and the more northerly grains, rye and oats, are of comparatively minor importance. If it were not for beer, most Americans wouldn't consume a pound of barley in a year. Wheat still holds pride of place in European farming, but potatoes, an import from the New World, compete strongly as dietary staples; and sugar beets and rapeseed, the latter used mostly to produce inedible oil for ethanol, account for major acreage. As in North America, barley, rye, and oats are marginal products used mostly to feed animals.

So what was it that recommended wheat and barley to the farmers of Pharaonic Egypt and Sumerian Mesopotamia? First of all, they grew wild in much of the region. Secondly, they did not require great amounts of water, and they could be planted as winter crops and thus avoid the torrid heat of summer. Thirdly, they preserve well. Wheat and barley kernels stored in dry places will keep for seven or eight years. But they were deficient as sources of nutrition, and their yields, in terms of calories per acre, were less than the yields of corn (maize), potatoes, manioc, yams, sweet potatoes, rice, or even apples. Moreover, corn kernels and dried beans last as long as wheat and barley, and even freeze-dried potatoes, the Incan *chuño*, and manioc can be stored for a year or more.

Unfortunately, the hot, dry climate of Egypt and Mesopotamia was not friendly to the roots and rhizomes that provided dietary staples in both the New World and Old World tropics. The same can be said of most tree crops. The tropics have scores of nutritious fruit varieties, but the first farmers in Egypt and Mesopotamia harvested few fruits other than dates, figs, and olives.

In sum, it can be argued that wheat and barley became the staples of the first Old World civilizations because they were the best crops available in a generally inhospitable climate, not because they were unusually delicious, nutritious, or especially suited to the purpose. The plant resources of the tropics held much greater potential for the high volume production of staple foods; and some plants, such as taro, bananas, manioc, maize, and potatoes, were cultivated in domestic form at least a thousand years before the rise of the Pharaonic and Sumerian civilizations. In other words, it was not the peculiar geographical availability of uniquely superior food crops that brought the first Old World civilizations into being. Those civilizations emerged in the riverine isthmuses of Egypt and Mesopotamia despite the fact that the plant resources of those regions were inferior to the resources of the tropics.

What About Herding?

Cattle herding might seem to offer a rejoinder to this conjecture about grain agriculture. It might be argued that setting oxen to pulling plows gave cattle-herders a clear leg-up toward civilization by making grain farming more productive. Therefore, maybe it was just an incredibly lucky thing that the people who domesticated wheat and barley lived in the same region as cattle, sheep, goats, and pigs, the cream of the crop among the allegedly tiny number of species worldwide that were susceptible to domestication. The problems with this construction of the history of human-animal relations are many, but four should suffice to illustrate the complexity of the considerations involved in studying domestication.[13]

1) There is no persuasive evidence that the large domestic animals we know of historically are the only ones that can be domesticated. This is because we do not know the process or processes by which any species became domestic. Though domestic cattle, sheep, goats, and pigs did come on the scene around the same time that people in the Near East began to cultivate wheat and barley, many animals were domesticated in later centuries in other parts of the Old World: donkeys in northeast Africa, horses and two-humped camels in Central Asia, one-humped camels in Arabia, onagers in Iraq, zebu cattle in Pakistan, water buffalo in India or Southeast Asia, banteng cattle in Southeast Asia, yaks in Tibet, reindeer in Siberia, and mithan or gayal cattle in northeast India. In the New World, the llama and alpaca are the only large animals domesticated in the pre-Columbian era, but caribou (*rangifer tarandus*) could

---

13. This section is explored more fully in my book *Hunters, Herders, and Hamburgers: The Past and Future of Human-Animal Relationships* (New York: Columbia University Press, 2005), 70–142.

have been domesticated, since they are the same species as the Old World domesticated reindeer. That New World caribou were not domesticated historically is conclusive evidence that every species with a potential for domestication was not domesticated in early times. Domestic animal populations appear in specific cultural contexts for specific reasons, not because certain people happen to be living in the places where there are species that take easily to human husbandry.

2) Research into the history of animal domestication increasingly indicates that cattle, a far-ranging and quite ferocious species in the wild, probably underwent at least two domestication processes, one in North Africa and the other in the Near East, perhaps Turkey. The African case rests on myriad images of cattle herders and their livestock in caves and on cliff walls in the middle of the Algerian Sahara, a region that dried up almost completely around 5000 years ago, and remains found at archaeological sites like Nabta Playa located deep in the desert about a hundred miles west of the Nile River in southern Egypt. The Nabta Playa site, dating back to the era before the emergence of Pharaonic civilization, preserves a megalithic stone circle that seems to be aligned according to seasonal astronomical phenomena along with ceremonially interred cattle skeletons.[14]

Though many historians write about cattle domestication as if people milked cows and harnessed oxen to plows and carts from the very start, the archaeologist Andrew Sheratt has convincingly argued that a thousand years and more elapsed between first domestication and the exploitation of what he calls "secondary utilities" like wool production, dairying, and draft harnessing.[15] However, the Saharan cattle herders, who moved south into the Sahel region as the desert expanded, never adopted plowing. But those who entered the Nile Valley did. This proves that here was no intrinsic relationship between grain farming and plowing during the period when cattle were being domesticated.

14. "Oldest Megalithic Astronomical Alignment Discovered in Egypt by Science Team," *Science Daily*, April 3, 1998, on-line at www.sciencedaily.com/releases/1998/04/980403081, recovered August 26, 2011.

15. The first of Sheratt's numerous writings on this subject was "Plough and Pastoralism: Aspects of the Secondary Products Revolution," in *Pattern of the Past: Studies in Honour of David Clarke*, edited by Ian Hodder, Glyn Isaac, and Norman Hammond, eds. (Cambridge: Cambridge University Press, 1981), pp. 261–306.

3) Cattle compete with humans for grain. Frederick E. Zeuner calls wild bovines "the crop robbers" in his classic history of animal domestication.[16] Wild cattle grazed on the fields of wild wheat from which the first domestic strain of the plant, a naturally occurring mutation that kept seeds from falling off mature stalks, was harvested; and they surely did not stay away from artificially cultivated fields as a favor to the first farmers. Indeed, as aridity increased and humans migrating from the broadening deserts to the isthmus river valleys became increasingly dependent on their grain crops, so did the wild cattle that were similarly being stressed by the changing climate. All the more reason for them to raid the earliest farmers' fields.

   As with other wild animals that came into conflict with humans, there were only three ways of dealing with the competition: eliminate the wild cattle through hunting, control them by domestication, or move them away from the endangered fields by herding. Hunting, as the expedition of Gilgamesh and Enkidu to kill the great bull of the mountains in the Sumerian *Epic of Gilgamesh* testifies to, eventually wiped out the wild species even as the image of the mighty fighting bull became a cultural icon. Domestication was accompanied by decreased size. Domestic cattle, zebus, and water buffalos were all substantially smaller than their wild ancestors in early times. Presumably this is because humans regulated what they could eat and kept them from the nutritious grain that they wanted for themselves. And herding encouraged nomadic human life-styles that came to be antagonistic to farming: the well-known eternal-conflict-between-desert-and-sown or cowboys-and-farmers-can't-be-friends motif. Despite the eventual harnessing of oxen to plows and carts, therefore, cattle proved more of a problem than an opportunity to the people who first undertook to cultivate wheat and barley.

4) An absence of large domesticates may have been a positive benefit to the precocious civilizations of the New World. In the absence of vast herds of grazing animals, which were present in temperate North America but absent in the tropics, crop growing may have been easier to undertake. Herding was neither possible nor necessary. Animal protein came from the sea and from the hunt. As for farming techniques, hand-planting of individual plants on prepared soil wasted less seed and produced higher yields than the broadcast sowing in

---

16. Frederick E. Zeuner, *A History of Domesticated Animals*, (New York: Harper & Row, 1963), table of contents.

open furrows that became standard in the Old World once plowing with oxen became commonplace.

The New World civilizations were also spared the ravages of diseases like smallpox and measles that are thought to have arisen from cohabitation of humans and domestic livestock. If those diseases decimated the populations of the New World after the coming of the Europeans, as historians generally suppose, but no longer felled so many European settlers because of acquired immunity, it is hard to imagine that immunity being acquired without catastrophic epidemics in prehistory when the cohabitation began. The back-filling with stones and/or brick of archaeological sites like Göbekli Tepe in Turkey and Nush-i Jan in Iran may have resulted from a desire to prevent any further habitation of places that had suffered devastating epidemics on the assumption that the site was somehow poisonous.

Conclusion

Colin Renfrew used the term "sapient paradox" to highlight the seeming problem of an immense time gap between the first appearance of modern humans in East Africa and the birth of the Pharaonic and Sumerian civilizations in Egypt and Mesopotamia some 5000 years ago. Those modern humans, as a species, he argues, were as capable of innovation and creativity as we are today. So why did they sit around twiddling their thumbs for tens of thousands of years before getting on with the noble tasks of building cities, inventing writing systems, devising temple rituals, establishing a division of labor, and conquering enemies?

As the beneficiaries of the worldwide culture that evolved from those first steps toward civilization, we have a difficult time conceiving of alternative pathways. Yet no one knew what civilization might ultimately achieve when the first strongmen applied themselves to commandeering the agricultural surplus of weak farmers and using it to feed the workers who toiled to build monuments to their glory and their gods. Most civilized Egyptians and Mesopotamians labored in the fields throughout their lives with little reward, while elsewhere in the world, and sometimes quite close at hand, groups of foragers lived healthier and more diverse lives involving far less work. None of the foraging peoples whose time and energy budgets have been studied by modern ethnographers, whether Amazonian Indians, Australian aborigines, or Pacific islanders, worked as constantly or as tediously to sustain their life-ways as did most grain cultivators in civilized realms down to the twentieth century.

We cannot be faulted for seeing our own modern culture as the best the world has ever known, but we can be faulted for failing to realize that this happy outcome would have been inconceivable 5000 years ago, and for failing to appreciate alternative paths of human development. Our dismissal of the urban civilizations of the New World as late, limited, and, worst of all, defunct, highlights these failings. Conventional thinking maintains that unlike the Egyptians, Mesopotamians, Greeks, Romans, and post-Roman Europeans, they just didn't have what it takes to shape the globe in their image. Incan roads, Olmec statuary, and Aztec pyramids astound, but for most of us they are cognitively cut off from the successful historical trends that we ourselves have benefited from. To be sure, it was the diseases that entered the New World along with the Europeans that killed off ninety percent of the indigenous population leaving empty land along with a vast array of cultural assets, from turkeys and tobacco, to potatoes and tomatoes, to chocolate and corn, for us to benefit from. The modern vegetable diet of humans around the globe derives more from the New World than from the Old.

So the crux of the "sapient paradox" is the question of why it took so long for humans, in their fully modern form, to become us. Posed this way, the hubris of the concept seems apparent. Nevertheless, it holds its ground so long as we look at the rise of civilization as a continuous and ever-expanding phenomenon from the fourth millennium BCE onward. That is why it is important to change our perspective and recognize the fact that the most precocious human populations, or in Renfrew's terms, the ones that most rapidly overcame the "sapient paradox," were in the New World, not the Old. The time gap between palaeolithic foraging and civilized pyramid building in tropical Peru and southern Mexico, was well over ten thousand years shorter than it was in the Old World. The modern humans there got to work doing the civilizational thing that we think our species was destined to do so much more rapidly than their slowpoke cousins in the Old World that it is impossible to believe that civilization building was in any way an intrinsic outcome of human ingenuity.

The isthmus conjecture that has been advanced here depends on two basic assumptions. First, when space is available for humans to spread into in response to population growth, group conflict, or even just a feeling of being crowded, they will instinctively strike out for new territory. It is worth noting that even today, most people respond negatively to crowding, and many of them dream of wide-open spaces. Second, when space ceases to be available, population growth will stimulate an intensification of food gathering, even to the point of plant domestication; and as population density continues to increase within a confined geography, intergroup conflict and/or cooperation will give rise to the differentiation of wealth, division of labor, exploitation of power differences, and construction of cities and monuments that we associate with the word civilization.

Application of these two assumptions in the isthmus conjecture leads to the following conclusions: There has never been a "sapient paradox." Civilization does not require more human innovation and creativity than the exploration of a new habitat and the acquisition of practical lore about its plants and animals. Plant domestication does not necessarily lead to civilization, nor is animal domestication essential, or always even favorable, to civilization. And above all, the history of the world should be written from a global point of view in which the peoples of the New World are recognized as the most precocious creators of urban civilization even it they were not chronologically the earliest.

Twentieth-Century History

(1998)

A S THE TWENTIETH CENTURY entered its final decade and no one had yet become hysterical about Y2K, a crisis some people imagined would erupt worldwide as computer programs failed to accommodate the shift from dates beginning with 1000 to dates beginning with 2000, the thought struck me that Columbia University Press should have its own entry in the inevitable contest to summarize the history of the century. As I mulled over such a project, it seemed to me that the way to make the Press version distinctive – dare I say better – would be to focus on the ways in which the fundamental conditions of human life had changed during the century rather than on narrating, yet again, the well-known master narrative: World War I > Great Depression > World War II > Cold War.

I proposed instead a thematic volume that would contain no explicit political narrative. I would give the authors of the twenty-three chapters only two instructions: to address both pre- and post-World War II time periods, and to give some degree of consideration to non-Western societies. The themes settled on were the following:

High Culture
Popular Culture
The "Woman Question"
Religion
Athletics: Play and Politics
Ethnicity and Racism
Imperialism and Decolonization
Nationalism
Socialism and Communism
The International Order
War: Institution Without Portfolio
Industry and Business

Money and Economic Change
Technology and Invention
Agriculture: Crops, Livestock, and Farming
Communications

Transportation
Scientific Thought
Paths to Discovery
Twentieth-Century Medicine
Ecology and the Environment
Cities
Demography and Population Movements

Recruiting contributors was a nightmare. Each topic seemed too broad. My greatest frustration came with the chapter on High Culture. I asked my colleague Edward Said to write it, and he declined. Then I went through a list of prominent names in the world of arts, letters, and music. They, too, declined. So I came back to Edward and urged him to reconsider on the grounds that there was no one better qualified than he to write such a chapter. He agreed that he was uniquely and superbly qualified. And then he said no again. So I wrote it myself, along with the companion chapter on Popular Culture.

Otherwise, I confined by work to editing and to writing an introduction and an epilogue. My introduction revolved around defending a thematic, as opposed to a narrative, approach to the story of the century. I compared my projected history with *Whither Mankind: A Panorama of Modern Civilization*, a book conceived of and edited by Charles Beard, who also taught in the Columbia Department of History from 1904 to 1917. Published in 1928, Beard's work contained these chapters:

The Civilizations of the East and the West (Hu Shih)
Ancient and Mediaeval Civilizations (Willem van Loon)
Science (Bertrand Russell)
Business (Julius Klein)
Labor (Sidney and Beatrice Webb)
Law and Government (Howard Lee McBain)
War and Peace (Emil Ludwig)
Health (C.-E. A. Winslow)
The Family (Havelock Ellis)
Race and Civilization (George A. Dorsey)
Religion (James Harvey Robinson)
The Arts (Lewis Mumford)
Philosophy (John Dewey)
Play (Stuart Chase)
Education (Everett Dean Martin)
Literature (Carl Van Doren)

Beard's goal was to substitute "a more cheerful outlook upon the future of modern civilization" for the "visions of despair" propounded by writers like Oswald Spengler in the aftermath of World War I. Unfortunately, the stock market crashed a year after *Whither Mankind* was published, and the possibility of a "cheerful outlook" crashed with it.

When I came to writing the epilogue to my own book, which appeared in 1998, I thought about the inevitability of predictive failure. Just as Black Tuesday reset the historical clock for Beard, the terrorist attacks of 9/11 did the same for the transition from the twentieth to the twenty-first century. My way of guarding against precisely this sort of bolt from the blue was to celebrate the unknowability of the future and the tentative nature of any master narratives purporting to be the story of our own times. Here is what I wrote:

Epilogue: The Twenty-first Century

The *Encyclopedia of the Future*, edited by George Thomas Kurian and Graham T. T. Molitor and published in 1996, is two volumes long and contains almost 500 entries ranging from "Abortion" to "Working Conditions." A crescendo of near-future scenarios is reaching movie screens and paperback novel racks. A new millennium at hand, futurology has become a semiserious profession. So many people, in fact, are already gazing into crystal balls that it would be foolish here to attempt to predict future events or trends. This chapter will confine itself, therefore, to the more modest goal of discussing how the history of the twentieth century may come to be rethought or reimagined from the vantage point of the twenty-first.

If the apocalypse is held in abeyance, one of the few sure things about the twenty-first century is that historians will chronicle its history, and that they will rewrite the history of the twentieth century while they are at it. Assuming the provisional, even evanescent, character of the various master narratives of twentieth-century history currently in vogue, this volume has concentrated on describing fundamental aspects of change in twentieth-century life that are arguably relevant to any approach to its history, giving no special consideration to any particular master narrative of this century's events. Behind this premise is the hope that what has been written here will continue to be germane to histories of the twentieth century written in 2050 or 2090.

Given the manifold rereadings and reinterpretations inflicted on the defenseless nineteenth century by twentieth-century historians, many of the most prominent having dedicated their careers to stamping into the ground the ideology and worldview of imperialism that guided so much historical writing before 1900, it must be assumed that many of our own points of view about the twentieth century will be augmented, if not entirely supplanted, by new ones devised to explain the roots of whatever comes next in the twenty-first. That is, the history of our own times and those of our parents and grandparents will, in large measure, be determined by the future, at least for the history-reading or history-viewing public that lives in that future.

The range of possibilities for plausible future rewrites of twentieth-century history is bounded only by the historical imagination, assuming that historians are somewhat more cautious in imagining times they have not personally experienced – whether long ago or future – than, say, science fiction writers. The following sampling of possible future master narratives of twentieth-century history is intended to illustrate the provisional and uncertain nature of our current understanding of our own times. They are couched in the form of proposals submitted to book publishers approximately a century from now – assuming there still are book publishers, and books.

The Asian Century: Twentieth-Century Foundations (possible copublication with Sony Publishing International)

Historians long maintained that the so-called American Century lasted from 1914, the beginning of the Thirty Years War, when the old order in Europe – the so-called "Long Nineteenth Century" – came crashing down, to 1991 when the United States, economically and politically enervated by its Pyrrhic victory over the Soviet Union, managed one last hurrah by leading a mighty international coalition against the pathetically overmatched forces of Iraq, a country less than a tenth the size of the United States.

This book proposes that the true story of the twentieth century begins in 1905, when Japan defeated Russia in the Russo-Japanese War. Despite the "ten-year setback" (1936–1945) of Japan's midcentury attempt to support its rapid economic growth militarily, the trajectory of Japanese economic growth was steady and inexorable, culminating in the shift of world economic resources to East Asia that is the central fact of our times.

Separate chapters will focus on the emergence of the "Little Tigers," and later the "Middle-Sized Tigers," that followed the Japanese road to prosperity; the saga of China wandering for decades in the trackless wasteland of imported European ideologies before finding itself economically at century's end; and the mysterious inability of Europe and the Untied States to solve the riddle of international economic competition. Similar special attention will be given, in the Americas, to the historic shift of influence from the Atlantic Coast, fatally infected by nostalgia for a lost era of European connection, to today's burgeoning Pacific coast.

Looking back on our amazing century of Asian development, it is important to brush away the petty historical details of European ideological quarreling – now so clearly perceivable as an irrational episode of civilizational suicide – and refocus public attention on the Asian twentieth century as the precursor of our own era.

The End of Nationhood: A Reappraisal

This book will examine a series of major writings from the late twentieth century from the standpoint of their assumption that the sovereign nation-state was an inevitable and irreducible component of human society. In light of the great wave of territorial realignment, political amalgamation, and internationalization of responsibility that has marked the last few decades, it is startling to see how little these developments were anticipated by the best minds of that earlier time. Captivated by a supposed seventeenth-century ideological watershed known as the Peace of Westphalia (1648), by which a handful of European principalities agreed to recognize one another's complete sovereignty within fixed borders, these twentieth-century thinkers ardently maintained the eternal verity of sovereign boundaries even in the face of events that were clearly leading to the demise of these archaic notions of sovereignty that we have witnessed in our own time.

The book will begin with a study of precursor movements in the earlier part of the century, notably what was called "communist internationalism" and the institution of the League of Nations. It will then discuss at length the lessons learned from the ill-fated United Nations, which represented the alternative to sovereign nationhood in the second half of the century. Special attention will then be given to concepts like "international sanctions," "humanitarian intervention," and "outlaw state" that emerged toward the end of the century as the theoretical equality of sovereign states clearly began to break down.

The entire argument will be set in the framework of the overarching role of non-sovereign worldwide economic organizations, both public (the International Monetary Fund) and private (AT&T), and of worldwide computer networking, with its intrinsic derogation of the concept of sovereign boundaries.

The Pacification of Hearts: The New World of Islam

In the name of God, the Compassionate, the Merciful

When the Messenger of God, God's prayers and peace be upon him, received into the community of Muslims adversaries that had formerly led armies and inspired hatred against God and His Messenger, he greeted them not with punishment and rancor, but with gifts and honors to pacify their hearts. So today, when God's providence, after long travail, has restored unity, power, and prosperity among His people, it is incumbent upon all Muslims to come to a new understanding of times past when Islam was despised and rejected by those who had temporarily gained a dominant position in world affairs. Only by such a revised understanding can we accomplish a contemporary pacification of hearts appropriate to the ever-increasing expansion of the Islamic community throughout the world.

The threshold event of twentieth-century history was the discovery of oil in Iran in 1903. God's providence decreed that the largest petroleum reserve in the world should be located in and around the waters of the Islamic Gulf, then known as the Persian Gulf; that, at the end of the twentieth century, Muslims would similarly control the second-largest pool of oil under and around the Caspian Sea; and, in our own century, that Muslims would gain preponderant positions in exploiting the vast petroleum reserves of the South China Sea and East Turkestan (formerly China's Xinjiang Autonomous Region).

Needless to say, the world transfer of wealth begun in 1974 under the briefly effective Organization of Petroleum Exporting Countries (OPEC) has continued, despite our wars, throughout this century. Our struggles, now thankfully over, have been over who would control this wealth and to what purpose. The sad story of European exploitation of Muslim oil reserves in the first half of the twentieth century was followed by the dual processes of Muslims gaining control of their mineral birthright, and Europeans and Americans jealously conniving to prolong their influence and, that ultimately failing, to cause oil wealth to be spent on Western goods. Western hatred of Islam became rampant, and hundreds of billions of US dollars (then the common international currency) were squandered on weapons aimed at fellow Muslims.

It was God's will that the great war between the believers in God's truth and what the Holy Qur'an calls the Imams of infidelity should have been fought within living memory. The abode of Islam having been divided against itself to the point of warfare, and those who command the good and suppress the forbidden having emerged victorious, the pacification of hearts must now be extended both to those Muslims who have rejoined the fold, and to the people of the West whose twentieth-century efforts to divide and dominate the Muslim community must be forgiven as desperate, fruitless struggles to avoid total energy dependency.

Success is from God, and victory is nigh.

Una Historia Nueva de los Estados Unidos/A New History of the United States (dual language publication)

Young Americans today look with pride upon the accomplishments of the United States of the Americas, the world's most productive the prosperous confederation of states. Sadly, however, few of them understand the history that led up to the Treaty of Mexico City in 2035. The purpose of this book is to relate the history of the twentieth century from the standpoint of that epochal event.

It will begin in 1898 with the Spanish-American War, the tangible beginning of Washington's unwavering determination, sporadically asserted since the early nineteenth century, to impose its will on the Spanish-speaking countries of the Western Hemisphere. Detailed examinations of the Platt Amendment of 1901–1934, legitimizing the Washington government's intervention in the affairs of Cuba, and the machinations surrounding the building of the Panama Canal (1904–1914), will illustrate government-level intervention. Discussions of the United Fruit Company, the International Telephone and Telegraph Company, and the Guggenheim family's exploitation of Chile's copper resources will serve a parallel purpose for business.

It will then narrate the struggle of the Spanish-speaking peoples living within the territory of the Washington government's jurisdiction to achieve personal respect, equality of opportunity, and language parity within a nation dedicated to denial of its multiethnic character. As amusing as late twentieth-century Latino and Chicano stereotypes (Charlton Heston as a Mexican in *Touch of Evil!*) may seem to today's youth, they should be reminded of the tenacity with which English-speakers defended the cause of language supremacy rather than brotherhood.

The trepidation expressed in 1994 – when the North American Free Trade Agreement went into effect – will be recalled as an example of the inability of some thinkers at the end of the twentieth century to understand the potential of a united American economic zone even as they were dreaming of unbounded progress (unfortunately never to be) deriving from peace between technologically advanced Israel and its labor-rich Arab neighbors.

In the spirit of multilingual fraternity and mutual respect that now pervades the American confederation from Montreal to Buenos Aires, this book will be dedicated to an increasingly prosperous future and stand as a warning against the hubris of one government or one people seeking hegemony instead of harmony.

After the Fall: Portents of Technological Dysfunction

If, at a propitious moment, as much brain power had been devoted to anticipating and forestalling the negative impacts of advanced technologies as to developing the technologies themselves, can anyone doubt that the world would be in much better shape today? I do not mean to suggest that key computer figures like Claude Shannon, John von Neumann, and William Gates should have been strangled in their cribs to prevent the proliferation of computers, or that as infants automobile magnates Henry Ford, Alfred P. Sloan, and Charles Kettering should have been put in a sack like unwanted kittens and dropped off a bridge to forestall the mass production of cars. Rather, I intend to question why twentieth-century thinkers took so long to recognize the hazards of new technologies.

Part of the answer, I will argue, lies in the time-tested human propensity to let immediate benefit outweigh eventual loss. Another part lies in the ideology of scientific progress that informed so much of twentieth-century thought, whether in the scientific laboratory or at the writing desk of a legion of speculative authors from H. G. Wells to Arthur C. Clarke. Late twentieth-century Cassandras, like environmentalists Rachel Carson and Paul Ehrlich, while heard, were invariably answered by a legion of learned defenders advocating future technological fixes for impending technogenic problems.

The bulk of the book, however, will examine the "greater fear" hypothesis, the notion that contemplation of a sufficiently calamitous catastrophe exercises a fascination that blinds people to presumed lesser dangers. While stories like graphic novelist Alan Moore's *Watchmen* (1987) or the film *Independence Day* (1996) explored the idea that invasion, or fear of invasion, from outer space might compel the nations of the world to set aside all differences, the end of civilization as we know it through all-out nuclear war became a far more common obsession from 1945 to 1991.

I will discuss imaginative permutations predicated upon nuclear catastrophe, from insignificant early literary efforts like Wilson Tucker's *The Long Loud Silence* (1952); to richly textured stories of civilizational regression like Walter M. Miller's *A Canticle for Liebowitz* (1959), Russell Hoban's *Riddley Walker* (1990), and Alan Moore's *V for Vendetta* (1990); to motion picture realizations like *Road Warrior* (1981).

The final chapter will focus on the birth, in the waning years of Cold War nuclear fear, of speculative fiction specifically devoted to technological dysfunction and environmental deterioration, including Neal Stephenson's *Zodiac* (1988), David Brin's *Earth* (1990), and Bruce Sterling's *Heavy Weather*

(1994). I will question whether the greater fear of nuclear annihilation engendered a reduced sensitivity to "lesser" dangers, or even a sort of longing for the worst to occur, thereby forestalling public outcry against runaway technologies until, as we now know, it was too late.

To proceed with this exercise would simply add more opportunities to demonstrate a complete misunderstanding of current trends. Hopefully, the overdrawn scenarios sketched above will not be taken as predictions of the future. Their purpose is immediate, not prospective. They are intended to illustrate a basic truth: that however well we think we understand the times we are living in, or the times just past, the future will surely belie these understandings. History can never be unchanging because it is more than the assembly and narration of past events. It embodies the writer's understanding of those events, and of the bases upon which he or she has assembled and narrated them. As people cannot avoid change in the course of their own lives, and across generations, so history cannot avoid change as stories are reassembled and rewritten under ever-changing circumstances.

It is often maintained that history has moved faster in the twentieth century than ever before. If this is so, master narratives should be falling by the wayside and new interpretations should be catching on with unprecedented alacrity. The legion of young historians currently embarked on research designed to overturn existing historical landmarks surely hope they are catching this accelerating wave of change.

One may as well argue conversely, however, that the "rate" of historical change should be judged by human factors, rather than by such mechanistic measures as increased speed of communication or transportation. Humans live somewhat longer now than in ages past. Possibly they go through the formative stages of life – adolescence, mating, reproduction, separation from progeny – a bit earlier or later. But fundamentally the human life cycle has remained a constant. Thirty years may see the passage of four generations of computer chip, but they still take an individual person only from infancy to adulthood.

Because there are more people than ever before, there are more human experiences than ever before. As the means of preserving evidence of human experience have vastly expanded through audio and videotape, motion pictures, and digital computer storage, the amount of information available for historians to digest is mountainously greater than ever before. How likely is it, therefore, that the impression of rapid historical change will be validated by the writers of history? Groaning under massive burdens of information, forced into narrower and narrower specializations by the magnitude of their task, and aware that society no longer pays much attention to professorial historians who write mostly for one another's edification, historians may well give place in the twenty-first century to journalists, moviemakers, novelists, literary theorists, or poll takers as shapers of opinion about times present or recently past.

This would be a sad circumstance, for historians know that change is slow, that the future changes the past, and that the present is hostage to the future. These are good things to know, and to remind people of.

Speciation and the Anthropocene

(2012)

I F THE HYPOTHECATION of a global era called the Anthropocene comes to be widely accepted, a wave of speciation may ultimately provide the best evidence of its reality. Over the time spans associated with geological terms bearing the suffix -cene, the current imbalance in the global carbon cycle associated with the onset of the Industrial Revolution may, in and of itself, prove too short-lived to warrant an epochal label signaling human agency on a geological scale. After all, unpredictable future changes in carbon emission and sequestration, for example, the advent of cheap and controllable fusion power, might well alter the measurements of atmospheric residues that have inspired the coining of the term.

However, the onset of an Anthropocene can also be associated with a vast increase in comparatively cheap and rapid interregional communication. Steamships and railroads inaugurated a trend that has steadily grown with little likelihood that it will suddenly cease or reverse course. These transportation changes, in turn, whether powered by hydrocarbons or not, have favored a massive relocation of living organisms, sometimes intended, but mostly unintended. The nineteenth century was the heyday of acclimatization experiments, as is well recorded in such organs as the *Bulletin de la Société Impériale Zoologique d'Acclimatation* published in the time of Napoleon III.

The "civilizing process" of imperialism generated myriad experiments in the transplantation of plants and animals. Rapid transportation contributed to this by shortening the time at sea during which the animals would have to be fed and cared for, and by making feasible a long-distance trade in animal products, such as beef from Argentina and lamb and wool from Australia. Most of the zoological experiments dealing with large animals failed, but bird life was profoundly affected on a continental basis. In New Zealand, for example, 137 bird species, mostly from northern Europe, were deliberately introduced during that period, and twenty percent of them became fully implanted.[1] In the United States, a project to introduce every bird mentioned in Shakespeare's plays gifted the country with starlings, among other spe-

1. Stephen A. Trewick and Gillian C. Gibb, "Vicars, tramps and assembly of the New Zealand avifauna: a review of molecular phylogenetic evidence," *Ibis*, vol. 152, p. 230.

cies. "The Acclimatization Society released some hundred starlings in New York City's Central Park in 1890 and 1891. By 1950 starlings could be found coast-to-coast, north past Hudson Bay and south into Mexico. Their North American numbers today top 200 million."[2] Fish, too, were transported to new ecosystems. Most notoriously, the gigantic Nile perch was introduced into Lake Victoria in the 1950s for sport fishing only to totally disrupt the lake's big-fish-eat-little-fish pattern and thereby cause the near extinction of several hundred indigenous species

As important as these deliberate introductions, however, have been the inadvertent arrivals of fish and insects, whose presence may be unnoted until they have already gained a foothold in their new environment. Sea lampreys, for example, may have benefited from the opening of the Erie Canal in 1825 to spread from their native habitat in New York's Finger Lakes and Lake Champlain to enter Lake Ontario, whence they further spread, thanks to changes in the Welland Canal in 1919, to the rest of the Great Lakes. A predatory animal, they have ravaged fish species at the top of the food chain, such as the lake trout of Lake Superior, and thereby changed the lake's entire ecosystem. Similarly, aggressive Africanized honey bees, also known as "killer bees," were inadvertently released into the wild from an experimental station in Brazil and subsequently spread throughout the Western Hemisphere, including into the American Southwest.

Some organisms travel in water tanks purged by ocean-going ships when they reach port. Others hitch rides with human migrants, tourists, and imported fruits and vegetables, or are brought into new lands, legally or illegally, as pets. When crossing the oceans was so expensive, slow, and dangerous that comparatively few passengers and cargoes were involved, and surviving long periods at sea without food provisioning was difficult, inadvertent introductions were less common. But the cheap and easy travel opportunities made possible by modern motorized transport, mostly fueled by hydrocarbons, have reversed that situation.

All of the above, both in general and in specific examples, is well known. What are rarely discussed, however, are the Darwinian implications of this wave of species translocation. "Darwin's finches," the dozen or so bird species recorded by Darwin among the fauna of the Galapagos Islands, evolved from a single species (not a finch, incidentally) that adventitiously found its way there from the South American mainland. It is generally agreed that the principle of natural selection caused various groups of the parent stock to

2. Steve Mirsky, "Shakespeare to Blame for Introduction of European Starlings to U.S.," *Scientific American*, May 23, 2008. [retrieved October 20, 2012 from online site www.scientificamerican.com/article.cfm?id=call-of-the-reviled]

develop specialized species-defining beak shapes adapted to particular food sources.

More recent elaborations on the principle of natural selection stress two things:

First, a small population cut off in some fashion from a much larger source population, for example by a sea level rise turning an extension of the mainland into an island, will share genetic traits in skewed percentages with respect to their distribution among the species at large. This creates a potential for sub-dominant traits in the parent species to achieve dominance and thereby come to characterize a new species.[3]

Secondly, species may remain static for very long periods of time only to experience episodes of rapid speciation when something like a climate shift fragments the population into small sub-populations that must adapt to new conditions of survival. This theory of "punctuated equilibrium" accords well with many fossil sequences.[4] Geologically attested extinction events, for example, are often accompanied, or immediately followed by a profusion of new species ramifying from previously stable species that survived the event.

If these widely accepted elaborations on the Darwinian principle of natural selection are sound, then it seems inevitable that the deliberate and inadvertent transplantations of species that marked the nineteenth century and increased still more, particularly in inadvertent fashion, in the twentieth century will eventually result in myriad new species. It may be that Nile perch, sea lampreys, starlings, and Africanized honey bees will remain stable and uniform species for centuries to come, but given the enormous number of instances of species translocation, it should be a near certainty that many translocation episodes will bring about comparatively rapid speciation, not simply in the form of species A developing into species B, but of species A providing a stem for a whole alphabet of descendant species.

Ironically, to the extent that animal species have played a role in thinking about the conjectural Anthropocene, it has been in terms of extinction, not speciation. Hand-wringing about the disappearance of wildlife, and less dramatically about the disappearance of domestic animal breeds, carries with it the tacit conclusion that future humans will live in much depleted ecosystems. Yet it could as well be argued that future humans will live in

3. For a brilliant discussion of how speciation relates to population size and geographical fragmentation see Ernst Mayr, *Populations, Species, and Evolution.* Cambridge: Belknap Press of Harvard University Press, 1970.

4. For the first influential exposition of this theory see Niles Eldredge and S. J. Gould, "Punctuated Equilibria: An Alternative to Phyletic Gradualism," in T. J. M. Schopf, ed., *Models in Paleobiology.* San Francisco: Freeman Cooper, 1972. pp. 82–115.

ecosystems that include many species of fauna and flora that do not yet exist.

This does not mean, of course, that some new kind of bear is likely to replace the polar bear. The species that have been most abundantly transplanted during the Anthropocene fall much more often into the faunal classes of birds, fish, reptiles, amphibia, and invertebrates than into that of mammals. Moreover, since it has been a commonplace to deride many intrusive populations as weeds, pests, vermin, or nuisances and to idealize the preservation of some "original" ecosystem, the prospect of a cornucopia of new lamprey species excites far less interest than the disappearance of a single antelope species.

Since the Anthropocene is defined as a geological period, and hence is presumed to characterize a period that will last for thousands, if not millions of years, it may be worth noting that many of the signature species of previous epochs began as small, unobtrusive organisms living among much larger and grander dominant species, which might have regarded them, if they were capable of regard, as pests or vermin. Mammals, for example, including humans, are descended from forerunners that were often as small as tree shrews. Could noisome feral pigs, over geological time, evolve into titanic beasts reminiscent of the giant mammals of the Ice Ages? Conceivably, but the greater likelihood seems to be that so long as humans directly or indirectly monopolize, or nearly monopolize, world consumption of food, the new species that will evolve from the torrent of translocations characteristic of the past two centuries will be small, perhaps even microscopic. But this does not mean that they will be insignificant parts of the global biome.

One additional note concerns domestic animals. Despite many generations of controlling and directing the development of breeds, zoologists are reluctant to recognize breeds as species. A chihuahua and a Great Dane are both dogs. But this may not prove to be an enduring situation, particularly among feral domestic populations in far-flung parts of the globe. Our current assumption that domestic animals will forever remain under human control – a source of despair for animal rights activists – may prove false, particularly if rejection of meat-eating or some other loss of utility leads to numbers of domestic animals being released or escaping from human control. Feral horses, donkeys, and in Australia camels already reflect, in part, a loss of the utility of those species for transportation. In using a term like Anthropocene, after all, we seem to be talking about geological time, not just the next century or so. If that should come to pass, then even the treasured class of mammals may generate significant additions to the world's roster of species.

Much of what has been discussed above applies as much to the many plants that have been accidentally or deliberately relocated to new environments over the past two centuries as to fauna, but domestic food plants pose an additional possibility. Many plants that have been genetically modified for purposes such as pest or disease resistance produce seeds that can be dispersed outside the bounds of the fields in which the crops are planted. "Feral" genetically modified plants, therefore, might contribute to a conjectural Anthropocene era of speciation analogous to feral domestic animals.

Compared with global warming, rising sea levels, fresh water scarcity, and mass extinctions, the likelihood of a wave of speciation may not currently warrant our concern. But if we are going to use the term Anthropocene to describe a geologic era touched off by human technologies, we should be aware of all of the evolutionary possibilities that such a term might entrain, and not just those that contribute to our contemporary penchant for predicting catastrophes.

The Last Millenarian Games

J UMPERS WITH FEATHERS appeared in the 24,675[th] Millenarian Games. The Commission should have seen them coming, of course, but that's always the way things seem in retrospect. Besides, where should they have drawn the line? In some of the earliest games, bigger muscles had been an issue, but the Commission hadn't done anything then. In the last analysis, no one could quarrel with bigger muscles. They were like bigger teeth. In events like the carcass pull, big muscles and big teeth made sense. How was the commission to know that not limiting tooth and muscle size would one day result in competitors thirty meters tall with teeth like stalactites?

They might, however, have ruled that jumping was a totally different kind of sport, one that inherently demanded closer regulation. In running a race, nobody much cared whether the competitors ran flat-footed, up on five toes, up on three, or on just one horny claw. Speed was the sole criterion. But in jumping there had always been arguments – never conclusively resolved – over whether the jumpers had to take off from one foot, or whether they could take off from two.

Proponents of the one-foot take-off maintained that jumping was simply a form of running in the air. One foot after another was the only way to go. Taking off from two feet, they said, wasn't jumping at all. It was hopping. But, of course, there were some damn fine hoppers eager to debate the other side. To them, it was beyond question that the spring they got from two legs would always be superior to what the running jumpers got from one. Excluding them would be obstructing the natural evolution of athletic excellence.

The curious thing, thinking back about the business of the feathers, is that arm flailing had peaked during the 340th Games and then declined. That was a long time ago, of course, but the stories that come down from that time tell about hoppers and runners hurling down the runway and then launching the jump with a wild flurry of arm movements. Some favored rotary. Some were up-and-downers. The theory was that pushing against the air with your arms would gain you a few millimeters of distance. Not much, maybe, but championships ride on margins like that.

Then short-armed guys started to show up, and arm flailing became as obsolete as gills. These jumpers had little bitty arms – and wouldn't you know it, absolutely humongous legs! – and when they tucked them in against their chests, they encountered so much less air resistance on the run-up that their take-off speeds wiped the long-armers out entirely. After that, the big-name coaches scouting for promising young jumpers began to offer the world to hatchlings with arms so little they could hardly keep their lunch from running away. Pretty soon, new world records were going to kids too young to rut.

Which brings us to the real mystery.

The feathered guys in the 24,675th had long arms. Real long arms. So just how did they get them? These stumpy little aerodynamic arms had been in for what ... twenty million years? Something like that. And now these guys come along with long arms. Forget the feathers for a moment. Just concentrate on the arms. Where had they been working out?

The buzzword that made the rounds among the insiders was "cross-training." The story was that the feather-boys had been working out with the divers. The divers! I mean, can you believe it? Sure, divers can *look* great falling off a rock. But how does that compare athletically with racing around a track or jumping for distance?

For that matter, how does diving compare athletically with disemboweling an herbivore? A diver can just open up and swallow a fish, but you've really got to work on your masseter, triangularis, and sternomastoid muscles to have any hope of getting to an herbivore's liver in under 30 seconds. Not to mention your trapezius. If you think gutting an herbivore is just teeth, go chew a palm frond.

Anyway, the story that went around was that by cross-training with the divers these guys had figured out aerodynamic ways of holding their arms besides folding them against their chests. Some guys said they had talked to guys – why is this sort of stuff always hearsay? – who had seen feather-boys diving with their arms sticking straight out from their sides, supposedly to give them more flexibility to maneuver during the fall.

So for me, the crucial thing in the 24,675th was the arms, not the feathers. At least that's what I thought then. "Feathers?" I said, "Feathers, smeathers." Sure I was wrong. But as I saw it, what hadn't folks sprouted from their skins over fifty million years? Long hair, short hair, long feathers, short feathers, scales – I hate scales – horny bumps, shells, red, green, grey: the only rule was, if it makes the gals ovulate, grow it. It was all surface. But sports is a matter of muscle, coordination, and skill. What pops out of your follicles isn't in the picture.

So there I was with these ideas that now seem prehistoric coming into the 24,675th. I could have laughed when I saw these long-armed guys with the feathers. There they were, running and hopping like crazy down the runway, hitting the rubber, and taking off. And what were they doing at the same time? You guessed it. Flailing their arms. DID IT LOOK STUPID!!

The Commission argued about it for millennia, of course, but there was no way of saving the games. First they ruled that "flying," as the feather-boys called it, was something different from a really successful long jump. On this basis, they barred flying from the games. You couldn't expect much else from commissioners with arms shorter than their jaws.

On the basis of the Commission's ruling, other athletes kept on training for the same old events. They even set some new records, especially in the mammal kill. Damn things were getting to be all over the place. But the old desire to hold the games just kept getting weaker and weaker. You can only run so fast, and jump so far, you see. And once the feather-boys started flying – my god, they were beautiful! – it just didn't seem to mean as much any more.

I guess you'd have to call it a paradigm shift. Sure, we could still produce hatchlings that would grow up to look like small mountains with muscles big enough to kick down trees and gut herbivores five times their size. But who wanted to? I mean, if you couldn't fly, why go on living?

I think when folks look back on this – and by folks I don't mean conceited feather-boys who've decided it's cool to call themselves "birds," I mean real folks, with proper tails behind them instead of bouquets of feathers – anyway, when folks look back on this, I'm not sure they'll understand why most of us have stopped laying eggs. Maybe by then they'll take flying for granted. How will they be able to understand what it was like to be there? Seeing the beauty of a world's end.